FRONTRUNNER INVESTING

TIME CHANGES THE RULES

James Bowen, PhD.

TABLE OF CONTENTS

Table of Contents

Table of Figures..8
Copyright..10
James' Foreword...11
Kudos for Frontrunner Investing.........................14
Nicole Verkindt...14
Feridun Hamdullahpur.......................................15
Richard Rémillard...17
About the Author...20
    Investor, entrepreneur, author, professor, inventor, media influencer, and community activist. 20
    Investor...21
    Entrepreneur...21
    Author..21
    Professor..22
    Inventor..22
    Media and Social Media Influencer.................22
    Community Activist..22

Dedication..25
How to Use this Book................................26
Part I..28
Chapter 1 Introduction................................30
    Investing can be Fun and Exciting..................31
    Securing One's Future......................................32
    Purchasing or Financing Another Goal............34
    New or Experienced in Investing.....................35
Chapter 2 Integrated Investing...................40
Chapter 3 Goal Based Long Term Investing........44
    Long Term Investing...44
    Strategic Investment...45
    Goals..45
Chapter 4 Time and a Disciplined Strategy..........50
    Many Investment Strategies.............................51
    Which Strategy is the Best?.............................54
    Data and Algorithms...55
    Common Strategies..57
    The Value of Time...58
    Years of Investing...59
    How Time is used by Different Investor Types..60
    Medium Time Horizon: Professional Fund Manager or Larger Scale Professional Investor....61
    The Advantage of Long-Term Thinking............63

    Predicting the Future..64
    Consider..65
    Risk vs Return over Time..................................65
Chapter 5 Invest in the Future................................67
    Trends..68
    Using Trends..69
    Themes..71
Chapter 6 Investable Themes................................73
    Excluded Themes..83
    Examples...86
Chapter 7 Cycles...93
    Cycles Lead to a Broad Timing Framework......95
    Why Does this Cycle Concept Work?...............96
    Traditional Thinking on Cycle Stages................98
    Cycles are like Ocean Tides.............................99
    Where are We?..100
Chapter 8 Risk..105
    Volatility as a Proxy for Risk...........................106
    Types of Risk..108
Chapter 9 The Emotions of Investing..................115
Part II...125
Chapter 10 Public Market Stocks........................127
    Finding Opportunities......................................127
    Creating Your Watchlist..................................133

Qualitative Assessment...................................137

Portfolio..140

Company's Position in its Industry..................144

Allocations..145

Volatility and Emerging Themes......................146

Winner and Loser Stocks..................................147

Buy/Sell...148

Selling/Re-balancing...150

Stop Order Strategies.......................................150

Risk vs Return Over Time................................151

Company Valuation Indicators.........................155

Information Sites...156

Chapter 11 Options Trading.................................159

Concepts...161

Selling Covered Call Options............................163

Selling Covered Put Options............................169

Repeated Selling Options.................................173

Other Option Strategies....................................173

Options Analysis and Strategy........................178

"The major fortunes in America have been made in land." John D. Rockefeller................................183

Chapter 12 Real Estate...183

Tenant Profile..184

It's a Business..185

    But Treat Tenants Well..........................186
    New House and Upgrades......................187
    Buy/Sell..187
    Return on Investment from Real Estate..........188
    Approximate Ratios.................................189
    Property Maintenance Policy..........................190
    Cycles in Real Estate............................190
    Your Team...192
Chapter 13 Start-up Companies........................194
    Finding a Start-up Company............................195
    Factors to Evaluate the Start-up Company.....198
Chapter 14 Gold and Silver................................205
    Gold..205
    Silver..209
    Gold and Silver...210
    Bullion...210
    Certificates and Streaming Companies...........212
Chapter 15 Coins, Stamps and other Collectibles 216
    Chapter 16 Bonds..220
    Returns: Stocks vs Bonds........................222
    Risk: Stocks vs Bonds.............................223
    Near Substitutes for Bonds........................227
    Chapter 17 Currency..231

Chapter 18 Integrated Strategy..........................233
    Investment Layers...233
    Measuring Success...237
    Using Cycles to Focus on Investment Types...240
    Investing as a Permanent Garden....................242
In Closing..246
PART III..249
Appendix A: Sites of Interest.............................251
Appendix B: Sectors and Business Cycles.........255
    Business Cycles..256
    Investor and Economic Impacts......................258
Appendix C: Additional Reading........................262
Glossary..264

Table of Figures

Figure 1: Compounded Average Percentage Yearly Return...59

Figure 2: Hours it takes to Double the Level of Human Information..74

Figure 3: Shopify and the NASDAQ 100...................87

Figure 4: Canopy Growth and the S&P500...............89

Figure 5: Microsoft Stock Price Compared to the Nasdaq 100..91

Figure 6: Risk/Return Cycles....................................97

Figure 7: Recession Dashboard.............................103

Figure 8 Developing a Watchlist............................130

Figure 9: Changes/Trends Happening...................131

Figure 10: Changes/Trends....................................131

Figure 11: Spectrum of Uncertainty.......................142

Figure 12: Portfolio on a Certainty Spectrum..........143

Figure 13: Industry Pipeline...................................144

Figure 14: Core Company in an Industry Pipeline..145

Figure 15: Volatility and a Stock's Life Cycle..........147

Figure 16: Options Analysis...................................178

Figure 17: Options Strategy Summary...................180

Figure 18: Historical Price of Gold............................206

Figure 19: Inflation Adjusted Historical Price of Gold 207

Figure 20: Gold vs Houses Returns in U.S. Dollars 208

Figure 21: Ounces of Gold per House......................209

Figure 22: Stocks vs Bonds Return..........................224

Figure 23: Stocks vs Bonds Risk..............................225

Figure 24: Risk and Return vs Time.........................226

Figure 25: Investment Layers...................................236

Figure 26: Deciding Investment Focus Among Asset Types..242

Figure 27: Economic Sectors...................................261

"If you're looking for a home run -- a great investment for five years or 10 years or more -- then the only way to beat this enormous fog that covers the future is to identify a long-term trend that will give a particular business some sort of edge." Ralph Wanger

Copyright

Frontrunner Investing by James Bowen, independently published

© 2020 James Bowen

All rights reserved. No part of this publication may be reproduced, distributed, or transmitted in any form or by any means, including photocopying, recording, or other electronic or mechanical methods, without the prior written permission of the publisher, except in the case of brief quotations embodied in critical reviews and certain other non-commercial uses permitted by copyright law.

Front cover image copyright by Commons Zero (CC0)

ISBN: 9781696028851

> *"Not money, not skills, but time is the biggest lever for massive wealth creation"* Manoj Arora

James' Foreword

I originally started writing this book as a means to record my personal strategy for investing for family members to read.

However, in conversations with people I would hear comments like

> *"I don't invest because its too complicated."*

> *"I invest, but my portfolio always seems to go down in value."*

> *"The stock market is really going up/down and I should buy/sell."*

> *"I don't have enough money to invest."*

> *"I'm young so I will invest closer to retirement as I have other uses for my money today."*

> *"I buy and sell a lot."*

In addition, I had the experience of talking about investing with a retired individual I had randomly met on a train. He had served in law enforcement and had a government pension. He had enough pension to live reasonably well but not such that money wasn't an issue. His investing approach was to read the prices of stocks on a public stock market information site and then invest in stocks that seem to be doing well, something similar to a momentum investor. Basically, his rationale was that if the stock price is increasing than it should continue to do so and investors should buy it before they miss out. In other words, he bought stocks based on "hot tips" and what everyone else was buying.

One stock he noted was a mining stock and it was doing well. He put a quarter of million dollars into the stock which was priced at $1 a share and then over the next while the stock price declined to 10 cents per share. A 90% loss for a person that just had enough pension to live a reasonable life style but not anything else.

I have also had conversations with individuals in the financial industry who are concerned with the low levels of financial literacy that some of their clients have and want to change that. The folks in the financial industry see bad financial decisions being made which are expensive over the long term and mean opportunities are bypassed. In order to have prosperous society, investment and financial security should be something everyone enjoys.

There are many books and sites on investing. I have often found that they have limited value as they don't start from the perspective of the average individual and their advantages (and disadvantages) but rather assume a higher level of analysis capability than the average person might not have. Other books are general in nature and while describing what one should do, they don't provide much information on how to make it work for an individual such as best practices. Best practices books tend to be a collection of ideas without a structure or way to understand how to apply them for the average investor.

This book is written for the investor that is looking for a structured approach to investing that can be implemented with the tools that the average person can readily access.

I hope the book benefits you.

Let's make the future better for all.

Financial inclusion is for everyone.

You can find James at:

LinkedIn: https://www.linkedin.com/in/bowenentrepreneur/

Best wishes

James Bowen, PhD, PMP

"Compound interest is the eighth wonder of the world. He who understands it, earns it. He who doesn't, pays it." – Albert Einstein

Kudos for Frontrunner Investing

Nicole Verkindt

"James provides a practical summary on investing, which makes it approachable for nearly any audience. His advice is clear, concise and focused on the long run, making this a great book for anyone, particularly those just starting out to create their long-term plan. I love this summary of trends and themes for the future, it was spot on to everything I am seeing in the start ups I support."

Nicole Verkindt

Star of TV Show Dragon's Den

CEO OMX

Star on Gimlet Media's "The Pitch"

Women Entrepreneur of the Year.

"When we own portions of outstanding businesses with outstanding managements, our favorite holding period is forever." Warren Buffet

Feridun Hamdullahpur

"Innovation is at the heart of building a thriving and dynamic nation. I've seen first hand how innovation keeps us competitive on the global stage and ensures our society is healthy and prosperous through the creation of new discoveries, new ventures and new jobs. It is imperative that we continue to invest in these opportunities. I believe that James hits the right cord in his advice and insights of the current state of investing and how investors can make investing part of their long-term portfolios. It not only will benefit them, but all of us."

Feridun Hamdullahpur, PhD,

President and Vice-Chancellor,

University of Waterloo,

Queen Elizabeth II Diamond Jubilee Medal

"You get recessions, you have stock market declines. If you don't understand that's going to happen, then you're not ready, you won't do well in the markets." Peter Lynch

Richard Rémillard

"I have read the book and liked it. It's written in a clear, concise style. And, it covers a lot of bases with much useful information. The author has done a fine job of probing into all the factors to consider when reaching for investing success. At its heart are some timeless reminders: invest for the long-term not for short-term asset flipping; diversify across various, uncorrelated asset classes; and, above all, do your homework. This book serves as a valuable addition to the literature on sound investing principles as championed by the likes of Benjamin Graham, Peter Lynch and Warren Buffett."

Richard Rémillard,

Executive-Director (2003-2014)

Canadian Venture Capital and Private Equity Association.

NOTICE

This book is intended to provoke your investment thinking. Please always seek the advice of financial/investing professionals before making decisions. It's your future. I would like to help, but your financial/investing decisions are your responsibility.

The author undertakes no liability or responsibility for the knowledge and information presented in this book. The author is not a financial consultant or certified financial expert.

The author has no vested interest in promoting any of the ideas or companies or individuals named in the book. The information is provided for your consideration, although at the time of writing the author might have investments in some of the companies mentioned in this book.

"I will tell you how to become rich. Close the doors, be fearful when others are greedy. Be greedy when others are fearful." – Warren Buffett

About the Author

Investor, entrepreneur, author, professor, inventor, media influencer, and community activist.

Dr. James Bowen is able to discuss an integrated strategic approach to investing in emerging themes for the long-term investor since his experience is both as an investor and a professional in emerging theme areas. He has a deep and broad understanding of innovation and creativity and how they impact society and the economy as well as how such ideas are translated into opportunities. He takes a strategic unbiased view of investing by anticipating how the future might shape out, how to take advantage of trends and changes and how investing goals can be accomplished in different ways. As such he isn't fixed on one approach but how they work together to implement high level investing goals.

Investor

James started investing at age 10 with his first savings bank account and savings bonds. Over the years he has invested in a diverse set of investment opportunities including mutual funds, ETFs, options, real estate, start-ups, stocks, bonds, silver, gold and collectibles. His investment experience covers recessions, market expansion and black swan events[1]. His focus has been global in both mature market and emerging innovation themes. He is a long-term investor, understanding the value of new ideas and how they will be implemented in opportunities.

Entrepreneur

At age 13 James developed his first computerized video game. At age 21, and while still in undergraduate university, James co-founded a software company. Over the next 15 years he and his co-founders grew an international client base. Since he left his initial start-up, he has co-founded 4 other start-up companies.

Author

James has authored or co-authored 4 previous books focusing on business topics such as entrepreneurship and technology. He has also authored or co-authored over 40 published papers on technology and business topics.

---

[1] Black swan events are unexpected ones.

Professor

He is or has been associated with 12 universities including 4 in Europe, generally focusing on new ideas. He has taught over 10,000 students at the undergraduate and graduate level in 400 courses over an 18-year time period. He has been a thesis supervisor for both Masters and PhD students. He has published papers on a variety of topics.

Inventor

He is the inventor of an underwater localization system using passive sonar, a task management system, an archaeological object localization system that uses ultrasonic and infrared, and 3 learning software simulation games.

Media and Social Media Influencer

Dr. Bowen has been interviewed on the internet, radio, magazine, T.V. and newspaper both in North America and Europe. His twitter account is on several curated lists. He has given many presentations and seminars on business and technology related topics. He does a frontrunner podcast series on technology and management topics and as well he is associated with an online blockchain radio site.

Community Activist

Community Interaction

James interacts with many students and start-up companies providing coaching and mentoring advice. He has also been a judge on many entrepreneurship competitions.

Social Initiatives

Ten years ago, James wanted to help change the entrepreneurial landscape and gathered 70 entrepreneurs to write two books describing their best practices on entrepreneurship. The vision of the books was to create funding and community support for a national entrepreneurship award that included both entrepreneurs and related community interaction.

At that time Startup Canada was forming and they undertook the herculean task to create an incredible national award program we now call Startup Canada's Startup awards. The award completed its 6th year and transitioned to its 2.0 version by merging with an existing national innovation award. This enhanced award program encompasses more of the new idea development process i.e. both the development of the idea (innovation) and its commercialization through start-up ventures. In addition, the enhanced award program has an associated charitable foundation.

With that established, James saw the next phases of the vision as incorporating the international element, large support companies and investment.

The FrontRunner Investing book is the first initiative on the investment side of the vision. The book introduces the reader to the value of long-time horizon investing on emerging themes created by new knowledge, innovation and trends. The book is accompanied by a discussion website for people to discuss long term growth opportunities.

We all benefit by investing in new ideas and growth areas.

You can find James at:

LinkedIn: https://www.linkedin.com/in/bowenentrepreneur/

Twitter: @jamesbowen2015

Website: www.frontrunnerinvesting.com

"if I had a way of buying a couple of hundred thousand single family homes, I would load up on them" Warren Buffet

Dedication

To my wife and children who inspired me to create a path to the future.

"If you're looking for a home run -- a great investment for five years or 10 years or more -- then the only way to beat this enormous fog that covers the future is to identify a long-term trend that will give a particular business some sort of edge." Ralph Wanger

How to Use this Book

This book has been divided into two parts. This first part describes a set of concepts that lay the foundation for a structured goal-based approach to long time horizon investing for the average individual investor. The chapters should be read sequentially to develop your perspective on investing and the necessary ideas needed around topics such as risk, emotions and emerging themes.

The next part of the book explores different investment types and can be read either sequentially or in a desired order. Each chapter in Part II provides a basic understanding of the necessary concepts around investing in the asset type along with practical suggestions to implement. At the end of Part II is the discussion on how to integrate investing in the different assets into one strategic structured approach that you can implement.

The third section of the book provides appendices for additional reading.

This book doesn't cover basic investing concepts and its recommended that you review basic ideas such as what is a stock or bond or option is from other sources before reading this book.

> *"People are so afraid of what they hear every day that they don't keep their eyes on the long term. The short term-ism of investors is what kills the long-term ability to compound."*
> Mary Callahan Erdoes

Part I

1. A long-term investment horizon can be used to our advantage.
2. Using a goal-based strategy, we can create a rational approach to investing and diminish the emotional approach to investing.
3. We can use themes of change happening in the economy and society and then find investment opportunities in appropriate asset classes.
4. Markets and assets tend to move in cycles so we can use the knowledge of cycles to our advantage.
5. Risk is the chance of losing money and we can take preventive measures.
6. We need to understand how emotions influence our thinking.

"Invest in yourself. Your career is the engine of your wealth." Paul Clitheroe

Chapter 1 Introduction

Welcome to this book on investing. In this book, we are going to explore a method for investing with a framework that is specific enough that the average individual investor can gain ideas for investing but first we need to know why you are reading this book.

Why are you reading this book?

- Is it because investing appears to be a fun and profitable endeavor?
- Perhaps you are looking to secure your future and look to investing as a way of doing that?
- Perhaps you have a specific financial goal in mind such as financing a new car or education or purchasing a house?
- Are you new to investing or have some knowledge and looking for an approach that will improve your current strategy?

Let's examine each of the above.

Investing can be Fun and Exciting

Generally, investing is time consuming and can be stressful. Even if we have a well thought out approach it's still possible to lose money and go through times when the returns on your portfolio aren't doing well compared to others or even compared to previous years. Indeed, it might appear that your financial goals won't be realized and with some investments you will likely lose money.

Some people are happy when their portfolio is doing well and depressed when it isn't. Linking your emotional wellbeing to the status of your portfolio is not a good idea. The market is comprised of many events, individuals and activities, most of which are out of your control. Thus, the current state of the market or your portfolio shouldn't be determining your emotional state.

If you're looking for a way to feel excitement and fun, I would suggest you do an activity where you have more direct control over outcomes and risk. Investing requires a control of one's emotions and isn't the place for euphoria or linking your sense of worth based on your portfolio's rate of return. When the market does well, and also your portfolio, it's not a time to feel smarter than others. Alternatively, when your portfolio is down, it's time to re-validate your approach, not a time to feel emotionally depressed.

> **Takeaway**
>
> Some of your investing decisions will be wrong.
>
> Some of your investments will lose money.
>
> Sometimes some or all of your portfolio will be in a negative position.

Securing One's Future

Securing one's future can be done in many ways. Some of these ways include having a suitable education for the type of career that works for you, moving to a location where jobs are plentiful, having a strong professional reputation, being frugal with one's expenses and saving money where possible. Perhaps some or all of the aforementioned are possible for you. Investing shouldn't just be your only way to secure your future.

Wealthy people generally know that to stay wealthy they need to live below their means; indeed, many self-made wealthy people stay that way because they are frugal. However, wealthy people also invest in ways to earn money either indirectly through their education and network building or directly though financial investments. Basically, investing needs to be one component of your overall life plan and aligned with other aspects of your life.

> **T**akeaway
>
> Prevailing wisdom suggests that we should set aside 5-10% of our income for investing.

We need to consider other aspects of our life when determining our approach to investing. For example, if one has a secure job (where the employer won't go out of business or lay off employees) then their approach to investing is different than for a person who doesn't have job security or a reliable income. This also has to be considered in conjunction with one's profession. Some professions are in high demand and a period of unemployment is likely to be minimal causing minimal impact on one's financial situation.

A person in a secure job such as a unionized environment or government job can anticipate that their income is predictable with a reasonable level of certainty. A person relying on bonuses or where the employer organization could cease to exist knows they might have periods of unemployment and thus need money to sustain themselves.

In general, the more secure your job is the longer your time horizon is and the riskier your investments can be. This situation is because your main source of income is secure and low risk. A person with a less secure environment has an interesting dilemma. They might look to their portfolio as a way of alleviating future income short falls. At the same time, since they don't know how long they might be unemployed and when that unemployment might occur, they tend to assume a shorter time horizon and less risky investments that are more liquid in nature i.e. because they might need cash quickly. This isn't always the situation. For example, a person who lives frugally and has a reasonable amount cash set aside or low debt might be positioned to withstand periods of unemployment or unexpected expenses and therefore be more tolerant of a riskier portfolio.

In summary, investing is part of your bigger life plan and other aspects of what you are doing financially. Each aspect needs to be considered in conjunction with the others. If you are in a profession that is in high demand or in a region with a great need for your skill set, then that offers some level of certainty around your financial security.

Purchasing or Financing Another Goal

In some situations, we might be using investments as a way of financing other assets such as a car or house. This approach can be problematic. In general, we might have a specific amount of money that we need at a specific time. This puts specific monetary and time constraints on the investment. Investment values tend to fluctuate over time, based on many difficult to anticipate external outcomes. As a result of values fluctuating, it might be worth considering an investment horizon shorter than when you will the need the money. A shorter time horizon might be preferred to reduce the risk of money not being available when needed and, in the quantity, needed. For example, if you know you will need money in 6 months then your investment horizon for that amount of money should be shorter than 6 months, possibly just a few months in order to accommodate for fluctuations in the investment market.

New or Experienced in Investing

If you are new to investing there are a lot of new ideas to consider in this book or any source of investing knowledge. Each idea in isolation isn't overly complex. What is complex is attempting to integrate all the ideas into one strategy that can be followed when decision making data uses incomplete or in accurate information provided to us about our investments.

I suggest that you also look online or obtain another source of information about the basics of investing. For example, what are stocks, bonds, mutual funds, real estate, and your region's tax and legal structures.

If you are experienced in investing then you might be looking to augment your strategy or have recognized that what worked in past might not work now and be looking for new ideas to test your implicit assumptions in your current strategy.

Questions we need to ask ourselves are:

1) When might I need money?
2) How much will I need?
3) How much notice will I have that I need money?

These questions are best answered by considering aspects of your life plan. It's the third question that is most critical. For example, if you might need money suddenly with little notice and thus will need to draw upon your investments, that's a different situation than for someone who doesn't have those realities. We will discuss the impact of this later in the book. For now, it could mean that you want a less volatile investment that can be quickly turned into cash.

Recommendation 1

Examine and modify other aspects of your life, if necessary and possible, to reduce the need for using your investments as a short-term source of money. Basically, if possible, structure your finances so your investments are not needed for a long time. Ideally sudden unexpected cash needs should be managed from other sources.

> **R**ecommendation 1 continued
>
> Basically, your approach should be that you wouldn't need your investment money for years and in a predictable way such that cash requirements can be planned over time. For example, you will have months before cash will be required and can thus plan an investment account withdrawal when it's optimal in the market.
>
> First invest in yourself.

We can look to other aspects of our financial situations by considering how we are using other assets or expenses. Consider the following personal expense decisions:

- When buying a depreciating asset such as a car/truck or boat only buy what you need. I often see people driving vehicles that are empty but for themselves, even empty of items being transported. Why does one need excess cargo space that is rarely used?
- Monthly subscriptions cost a lot over time. Which monthly subscriptions are not needed or can the same service could be bought with a 1-time acquisition? This question can include a variety of services.
- With depreciating assets consider the maintenance, energy, insurance and frequency of use of the asset. With assets that we use

infrequently it might be better to do a short-term rental. For example, rent a sailboat if one only sails a boat for a few days or so a year, or rent a car when travelling out of town and buy a small car for in-town travel. If you use a vehicle infrequently consider the value of ride sharing or using a short-term rental car i.e. that rents by the hour.
- Is it possible that people you know are also interested in buying the same items you are and thus can combining purchases result in a group discount?
- It is possible to get many services for free, for example, long distance calls, and shipping.
- If you own a depreciating asset consider selling it or renting it to others.

"If you buy things you do not need, soon you will have to sell things you need." Warren Buffet

Summary

- Know why you are investing. It shouldn't be for emotional gratification. We don't invest for bragging rights or to feel smart.
- Ensure that your complete financial, professional and life plan are part of your decision to invest.
- Your first step is to invest in yourself by aligning your career, lifestyle and other life decisions.
- Structure other aspects of your life such that you will not have a sudden and immediate requirement for money from your investment account.
- Divest of excess depreciating assets.

"The single greatest edge an investor can have is a long-term orientation" Seth Klarman

Chapter 2 Integrated Investing

In this chapter we want to describe integrated investing and how you can use various asset types to your advantage.

There are many possible investment types, such as:

- Gold and silver
- Currency including crypto currency
- Public stock market companies
- Public stock market options
- Bonds
- Collectibles
- Real estate
- Private equity investing through a venture capital company or as an angel (also referred to as dragon) investor
- Private lending and syndicated mortgages
- Other non-liquid assets such as vending machines
- Gig (side hustle) economy activities

Each has its own possibilities and approach. There are many books available that discuss investing approaches for each of the above asset types but few (or none) that discuss investing with those asset classes as part of an integrated approach.

This book wouldn't replicate the detailed procedural discussions available in other books for the different asset types. For example, if you are investing in real estate you should get a source of information that discusses the local legal, tax and reporting procedures for your jurisdiction.

Similarly, there are many books that present best practices for stock market investing that have been learned by practiced investors. These books describe the approaches of individuals such as Warren Buffet or Peter Lynch. There are also books that discuss the results of empirically tested theories and then reveal insights gained such the Efficient Market Hypothesis that can be used to guide strategic thinking.

I would also recommend that you obtain sources of information about stock options and currency to understand the nuances of each.

This book assumes a background knowledge of stocks and bonds, etc. along with an understanding of the process of buying and, selling assets and, their tax and legal implications.

What we want to discuss in this book is an approach which takes a more integrated or system approach to investing across a variety of asset types.

Integrated investing means to disperse your investments across different asset classes to decrease risk and take advantage of the natural cycles of each asset class. We can take advantage of cycles by buying the most appropriate asset type when its most opportune.

This means having the ability to buy, sell and move money between asset types when needed.

Recommendation 2

Have your tax, legal, bank and investing accounts structured so that you can easily and optimally flow cash between different investment types when needed. This might involve developing a team of experts and sources of information to understand tax, legal and other information on asset types if needed.

Summary

- Integrated investing is an approach to invest across different asset types that takes of advantage of their natural cycles.
- Structure your financial accounts to provide the potential to move money between asset types.
- There are many asset types and its worth understanding them and using them as part of an integrated investing approach.

"If you aren't thinking about owning a stock for ten years, don't even think about owning it for ten minutes." Warren Buffett

Chapter 3 Goal Based Long Term Investing

Long term investing wins over time[2]. In addition, following any investment strategy wins vs not following a strategy. Not following a strategy depends on luck, perhaps investing based on emotion and generally following an adhoc reactive approach. As described below there are many investment strategies.

Long Term Investing

In the previous chapters we introduced that the optimal situation for the average person (sometimes referred to as a retail investor[3]) is to have a long-term view of investing. We define long term investing to be

---

[2] This guide assumes a long-term investing approach where investments can be held for indeterminate lengths of time and need to sell an investment isn't fixed to a specific date or even range of dates.

[3] A retail investor or average investor is an individual that invests their own money and typically doesn't do that as their profession or is not part of a wealth management organization.

measured in years, preferably decades. This has significant consequences that we will explore in this chapter.

Over time, long term investing can be successful given a structured strategy. In this chapter, we need to describe a long-term investing strategy in a way that gives you the confidence in its potential such that some of the emotionally draining episodes of market volatility don't cause emotional reactive investment decisions.

Strategic Investment

By strategic we mean a structured approach that can be implemented. As such we need to have information that determines our current state, our desired state and a rational approach to make decisions.

Note, the definition doesn't include gambling or emotionally based decision making but instead uses an approach based on rational logic and frameworks for decision making.

Goals

Let us first describe what we are attempting to accomplish by investing over the long term. While sudden and significant increases in wealth might be desired, outside of winning a lottery, a sudden increase in wealth is rarely achievable. Incidentally, winning the lottery and other forms of gambling are a form of luck, and, luck isn't controllable or dependable. We don't want a strategy that depends on luck. We want a strategy that focuses on the following 5 goals:

> ### Your Portfolio's 5 Goals
> Global, growth oriented, consistent, diverse, and recession/downside/risk resistant.

In this book, we will explore a strategy that fits those key goals.

Global: Generally, the US market is a prime market for growth and there is a reasonable argument for diversifying across regional boundaries, however, global companies have customers in a variety of locations. As a risk reduction approach, we want to see that companies have a customer base in a variety of geographical locations. We can still have investments drawing income from only one region but we want to see in our portfolio income from a variety of regions.

Growth Oriented: There are a number of possible strategic approaches to investing such as momentum and value based. As we will explain in a later chapter, the growth-oriented approach has its advantages and will be the focus of this book.

Consistent: Having our portfolio with wide fluctuations might not be a problem over the long term if the portfolio consistently increases in value. We might have times in which the portfolio isn't doing well, or some individual investments have bursts of significant gains or losses. We need to recognize that individual investments and our portfolio can fluctuate given the natural cycles/rhythms of the investment type and economy. However, over time the portfolio should have a consistent return on investments. That time duration could by bi-yearly or even every few years but we wouldn't expect consistency over time periods less than 1 year.

Diverse: Generally, by diverse we mean investment types that aren't significantly positively correlated. If two assets or asset types are positively correlated then a decrease in an asset type or individual asset could impact all the correlated assets. For example, a lack of diversification means having asset types that derive revenue in the same:

- o Geographic region

- Customer type
- Economic situation
- Business model
- Certainty of future return on investment

Diversity of investments links to the risk profile of the portfolio and we will see that idea again in the section on risk later in this book.

Recommendation 3

Some investing literature will group technology companies as a correlated asset type. However, many technology companies have different business models, customer types, product/service types and geographical regions. Any discussion that groups investment in technology companies/industry as a single investment type should be considered skeptically. The stock market might treat technology companies as one sector but they should be considered separately.

Recession/Downside/Risk Resistant: Downturns in the value of an asset type are a natural part of the economy. In addition, individual assets can have downturns. Indeed, individual assets can go to a zero value. Assuming that the downturn isn't indicative of a deeper issue, then over time losses from downturns can be recovered.

In general, a recession might last between 12-15 months so a decade long investing time horizon has time to recover.

However, a recession or downturn does need that time to recover. For example, a 10% downturn takes an 11% upturn to recover the loss. In general downturns such as recessions are difficult to predict however we can anticipate that they will occur. We can't completely protect against downturns but we can lessen their impact. In addition, as will be discussed in a later chapter we can take some advantage of downturns.

Summary

- **A goal driven investment approach gives us a way to objectively measure our progress and it's the start point for a rationale investment strategy.**
- **The goals discussed in this chapter indicate both the basis for an investment strategy but also the basis for some downside protection and risk mitigation.**
- **A goal driven approach helps remove some of emotionality of decision making in investing.**
- **Having goals also provides us a way to measure results.**

> *"The trick is not to learn to trust your gut feelings, but rather to discipline yourself to ignore them. Stand by your stocks as long as the fundamental story of the company hasn't changed."* Peter Lynch

Chapter 4 Time and a Disciplined Strategy

A losing approach is emotionally reacting to market news or trying to time the market with frequent buying and selling of an investment, particularly a stock. Other losing (negative) approaches are buying something because everyone is buying or that someone has suggested it as an investment to you. A suggestion on an investment could be useful if it aligns with the strategy one is using and we still need to do our own research on the opportunity.

Those approaches aren't a strategy but more akin to gambling or relying on luck. As previously mentioned, luck has little element of control and can severally impact our emotional state if the investment doesn't appear to be doing well. We need the emotional fortitude of a strategy so that we can know why we investing in a particular asset.

Knowing the why gives us strength to weather the downturns and guidelines for when its time to sell.

We want to choose a strategy that has rational decision guidelines and that works with the information and analysis tools that we have.

> Takeaway
>
> There exist many investment strategies. Two key points are:
>
> Different investment strategies require different information sets and analysis capabilities.
>
> A winning investment strategy might not always win all the time.

Many Investment Strategies

Value Investing

Value investing is a strategy most notably practiced by Warren Buffet. It essentially looks for companies that are priced below their intrinsic value[4]. Value investors believe that stock market investors can over react to news and economic conditions. As a result, a company could be priced below its value. Eventually

---

[4] Intrinsic value is a combination of using financial analysis such as a company's financial performance, revenue, earnings, cash flow, and profit as well as fundamental factors, including the company's brand, business model, target market, and competitive advantage. Financial metrics might include price to book and price earnings ratios.

other investors will realize the mistake and the stock's price will return to what it should be. This misalignment creates an opportunity.

However, there are two issues to consider. First is whether value investing is still as feasible in today's environment where information is readily available. The Efficient Market Hypothesis suggests that there can't be any advantages because all information is available to all individuals at the same time. There are counter arguments to the Efficient Market Hypothesis that suggest human psychology and other factors will create a misuse or ignoring of information and thus create misalignment opportunities.

Price discrepancies shouldn't occur. However, studies of investing do suggest that people over and under react even given the same information. Perhaps this is because some investors have a volatility-based investing approach.

A second consideration is the "Value Trap" which is when an asset appears cheaply priced relative to its intrinsic value but in fact it's priced appropriately because its value is actually low. A value-based investor has a challenge to differentiate truly underpriced stocks from the ones that appear to be priced low but are actually not.

Volatility Investing

Buy on the rumor and sell the news is a common motto. It suggests profiting from volatility in an asset's price. Such investors look for achieving gains when an asset's price oscillates perhaps as large number numbers of investors invest or divest thus causing greater oscillations. This tends to a short-term investing approach.

Growth Investing

Growth based investing is a strategy to focus on growth-oriented companies. Such assets might not have a stream of income such as dividends but are more oriented to capital gains. An issue with this strategy is determining the value of an asset whose future is unknown.

Momentum Investing

This style of investing looks at assets that are currently undergoing rapid price increases and seeks to profit by that increase.

Dividend Investing

Typically, a dividend paying stock's value increase is partially due to capital gains and partially to dividends. The dividend strategy investor looks to companies that are increasing their dividends over time, i.e. the ones with consistent and significant dividend increases over time. They consider companies that are increasing their dividends worthwhile investments and that also partially insulates the investor from stock price downturns.

As we see there are many different investment strategies and many more not discussed in the above section. However, a key point is that they rely on different information sources, analysis, knowledge, and, they might not always work. Typically, a strategy might need certain economic conditions for it to work. For example, during a depression a growth focused strategy might not work over the short term, or during the emergence of a new industry a value-based approach might be less effective.

Which Strategy is the Best?

While particular investment strategies can work well in given situations and some work well in many situations, we might be tempted to ask which works best?

To answer that let's consider the game board Monopoly where there is generally one winning strategy: accumulate more properties and hotels then anyone else, eventually the rent cost to the other players becomes ruinous. With investing there are many strategies, its not like the game of monopoly with one strategy and we are in a winner take all competition.

A better way of thinking of it is similar to asking the question which form of exercise is the best? The answer is usually the form of exercise that a person is motivated to do regularly, is applicable for their situation and improves their overall health. Some people do better as swimmers and some as walkers. Or we could ask which profession should one do to be the most prosperous. The answer depends on the individual's life circumstances and how motivated they are and what they are doing in other aspects of their life. Choosing a strategy needs to align with one's ability, motivation, risk tolerance, etc. Rather than asking which strategy is best we need to ask ourselves what data and analysis capability do we have, what fluctuations in values can we tolerate and what is our time horizon.

Data and Algorithms

Modern trading by professional investors is done by automated computers using sophisticated algorithms that adapt and evolve over time. These computers have access to a wide variety of past and current data types. Indeed, the trading algorithms can be using better data than the executives at the company whose stock is being traded.

Its unreasonable to think that an average person without access to such systems could do better than that professionals.

So that leaves a few options:

1) Invest differently, for example, buy when the algorithms are selling and sell when the algorithms are buying. In other words, a contrarian approach.

2) Use a different time horizon and perspective. In other words, a longer time horizon which is future oriented.
3) Invest in existing ETFs, index and mutual funds that use such sophisticated data and algorithms.

Passive Investing Using ETFs

Passive investing using Exchange Traded Funds (ETFs) is a significant investing structure for many people. ETFs have gained great popularity over the last few years. ETF companies buy a portfolio of funds and then the investor can buy units of the ETFs.

While ETFs themselves are not similar to the strategies we just discussed, they are a significant way to implement a strategy. ETFs are typically based on an index which is a defined description of some segment of the market, such as companies of a certain size or region or perhaps the Standard and Poor (S&P) 500. The ETF company then buys company stock that matches the index description.

By choosing an ETF, one can implement a strategy, for example, dividend paying large US companies. Typically, an ETF focuses on medium to large companies and must wait until an index has been defined. If you are interested in obtaining the returns generated for a particular region, industry or even the market as a whole, then investing in ETFs might be the solution for you. For example, the US stock market as a whole tends to average around 7%

a year over time. If that rate of return is satisfactory for you then the best approach is to buy some ETFs and your research and investing work is done. For example, you could buy an ETF for the S&P 500 and one for the NASDAQ technology index and be done. This two ETF approach will give you the broad US market and the growth potential of technology companies. ETFs are a simple and generally an effective way to invest.

Although ETFs do suffer from a herd mentality, if everyone is investing in them its possible that opportunities in the market not represented in an ETF will be overlooked. In addition, that profits of ETF will revert to the mean (average) since everyone is focused on a similar investment strategy.

Common Strategies

An investing strategy that is well documented is where each investor uses the same data and algorithms. Then the profit potential is diminished as each investor makes a similar decision and invests in the same opportunities driving up prices and reducing profit potential. Using a strategy that larger investors use could mean its profit potential has been squeezed out by so many investors usually in favor of the large investors.

Takeaway

> It's possible to use different strategies as appropriate for the situation and also to combine elements into a strategy that uses time to its advantage.
>
> Investing in an ETF approach is applicable for many people.

The Value of Time

Time is an investor's greatest advantage. You are likely well aware of the value of compounded earnings. The concept is simple and states that earnings earned on previous earnings increase the overall portfolio more quickly. For example, if we earned 10% in year one on $1 then a year later, we have earned $1.1 and then if we earn 10% in year 2 then we have earned $1.21 or on average 10.5% per year, as we see in the following figure.

The following figure displays a consistent yearly 10% return on an original $100 investment. The returns are compounded each year, in other words each year's return is added to the portfolio total and then the new total invested to increase another year's return. If we take the yearly return and average it, notice how the average return increases over time on the original $100. By year 10, even though the portfolio is still earning 10% it's now earning the equivalent of a 15% return on the original $100.

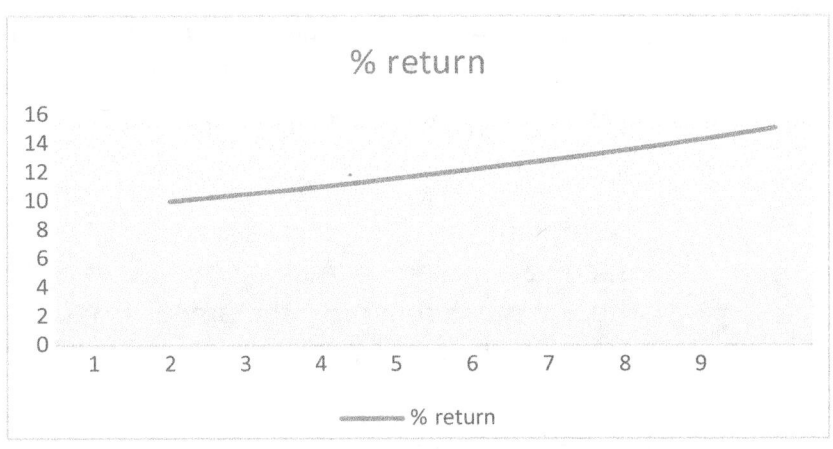

Figure 1: Compounded Average Percentage Yearly Return

Figure 1 illustrates the following concepts:

1) Consistent returns are of significant added value over time.
2) Earning returns over longer time periods works significantly to our advantage.
3) We don't have to pursue high risk investments to get high returns if we use time to our advantage.

Years of Investing

The more years we invest the greater the potential to generate viable wealth. Assume a 6% rate of return and monthly investments.

If you start saving when you are 20 years old, you'll need to invest $319 a month to earn one million dollars in 47 years at age 67.

If you are 40 the required monthly investment amount increases to $1,240 to reach one million dollars in 27 years at age 67. That's almost quadruple the amount than if you had started saving at 20.

> Recommendation 4
> Use time to your advantage.
> Invest early and keep investing.

How Time is used by Different Investor Types

Given the importance of a time horizon in an investment approach, let's consider two general time horizons in addition to the long-term investor approach described earlier.

Day Trader: Shortest Time Horizon

A day trader is a person who is continuously buying and subsequently selling financial instruments within the same trading day, such that all positions will usually be closed before the market close of the trading day. Depending on a day trader's trading strategy, trades may range from several to hundreds of orders a day. A day trader tends to use large data sets and algorithms to make trade decisions. For example, they look for small price movements and anticipate where the movement will take the stock in the next few seconds or minutes. Their goal is to make many trades with small profits from each trade.

The percentage of day traders that lose money has been estimated to be between 55% to 90% so it's not a consistent strategy that is readily doable for the average retail investor.

Medium Time Horizon: Professional Fund Manager or Larger Scale Professional Investor

A professional fund manager manages money on behalf of other individuals (or manages their own money) which tends to be in large sums. Similar to day traders they tend to have access to large data sets and algorithms. Their time horizon might be measured in yearly quarters or years. Professional managers are under pressure to deliver increased returns for each reporting period. While their time horizon is longer than day traders, they are still time pressured to deliver returns, and will seek out the mechanisms to deliver the returns perhaps even seeking risker assets as a way to meet their time base profit goals.

The difference in time horizons, data sets and use of algorithms drives the type of strategies used by each of the two-time horizon investor types. Understanding that different strategies and time horizons tend to focus on different decision-making approaches is critical.

A long-time horizon investor can use the disadvantages that short or medium time horizon investor has to their advantage by using tools that work best for their approach.

> Takeaway
>
> Sometimes we read of success a particular investor has or some of their best practices. Sometimes the advice we read doesn't explicitly discuss the assumptions or strategy inherently being used. Thus it's possible to be misled because we might not realize that the advice won't work well for the average retail investor. Reading about a best practice without placing it within the context of its associated strategy can be misleading.

> Takeaway
> Using a long-time horizon strategy gives advantages over short time horizon investors (which we discuss in more detail later). For now, consider the following:

> - Long time horizon investors can use risk and volatility differently than investors with a short time horizon.
> - We can take advantage of situations that short/medium term investors can't.
> - We aren't under the time pressure that short/medium term investors are, so we aren't pressured to make short term decisions that are detrimental to the long term.
> - We can interpret market events differently.

The Advantage of Long-Term Thinking

Large institutional funds, day traders and other professional investors tend to have a few weaknesses that long-term investors can use to their advantage. Short and medium time horizon investors tend to focus on companies that have years of historical data, they are quarterly focused, they don't want to take risks with unknowns so it's safer for them to buy well-known companies. In addition, big investors have algorithms, data and expertise that the average retail investor doesn't have. Also, large investors tend to focus on large opportunities, small opportunities are too small.

Long term investors don't need to use the data and algorithm intensive strategies of professional investors. Instead long-term investors can focus on emerging themes, and, smaller investment opportunities where quarterly returns are not as important as long-term potential.

Predicting the Future

In the financial and business news media we are inundated with news that continuously makes predictions of the future or a possible future that could occur. For example, if a certain event occurs then it could mean another event might occur. However, there are two things to keep in mind:

- The patterns of the past as represented in the economy. For example, the types of industries, companies and investment approaches have changed over time so patterns of events that occurred in the past are unlikely to occur again in exactly the same way. Over the last few decades we have seen a shift to a service-based economy and the emergence of new industries such as social media. Thus, each recession tends to be triggered by a different series of events and past recessions aren't exactly a pattern for predicting future recessions.
- There is great benefit gained for being the one to predict the next significant event, so lots of events are predicted by would be investor gurus, but no one remembers the predictions that didn't happen.
- The media need to report news every day that captures viewers/readers attention so a barrage of conflicting information of negative news and positive news is constantly given. An example of this would be predicting recessions

and expansions of the economy in different articles on the same day.
- Most of the information given on the business and financial news is more targeted at the short to medium term investor than the long-term investor.

Recommendation 5

The financial and business news that is speculative and/or predictive in nature is not dependable. As such, it's best to not take much heed to it as we will discuss later in the book.

In addition, using a strategy that doesn't require unreliable emotionally charged information is better for the average retail investor.

Consider

The venture capital company Andreessen Horowitz that invested in Skype, Facebook, AirBnB, Stripe, Twitter, Groupon and Foursquare has a 7-10-year time horizon when making their investments.

Risk vs Return over Time

In chapter 16 on bonds, I provide an analysis of risk vs return vs the investor time horizon for bonds vs stocks.

Summary

- When investing, a strategy beats not having a strategy.
- A strategy gives us a rational approach that should temper impulsive emotional investing.
- A strategy means we won't invest based on "hot tips", luck or other forms of speculation that are not based on some form of evidence.
- There are many strategies. Some strategies are more data and algorithm intensive and have been used to the extent that the average retail investor is at a disadvantage in using them.
- Time is an advantage that the average retail investor can use to build an approach that doesn't compete against the larger professional investors.
- Most of the financial and business news in the media is targeted to short/medium term investors.
- We can't predict the future but can use time such that risk and volatility can be used differently over a long-time horizon.

"Invest for the long-term." Lou Simpson

Chapter 5 Invest in the Future

As mentioned in the previous chapter, the economy and its structural elements are undergoing constant change. In addition, society's needs and wants are changing. We are in an era of change rarely seen in the past. Over the last few decades innovation has been a significant driver of change. Technology has provided a platform of possibilities for new services, products and business models.

> **Takeaway**
>
> Innovation/invention has progressed to the point where there is a convergence of technologies and knowledge. Such a convergence means that the pace of change is increasing with a multitude of new opportunities occurring as each new change in society/economy creates a new set of opportunities.

We can't know the future but we can invest in themes or major changes happening in the economy/society created by new knowledge and new innovations (i.e., blockchain), industry (i.e., renewable energy), customer perspectives (i.e., healthy eating) and business models (i.e., mobile vs in store shopping).

Trends

Trends are a series of occurring events, activities or perspectives that are changing some aspect of society, industry and/or the economy. We can separate events, activities and perspectives, as follows:

> Activities are actions that people or other living organisms can undertake.

> Events are outcomes resulting from an activity or series of activities that have happened. Events could result from many possible actions that living beings undertake or through other forces such as weather, erosion, lightening, etc.

> Perspectives are what people consider to be acceptable or not and, what they consider to be important or not.

It is the activities, events and perspectives that define trends. Trends progress at different speeds, their significance varies, the ability to detect them and the ability to profit from them tend to differ.

Takeaway

> We can look for trends and use their potential to align with innovation and knowledge to create change and opportunities that need investment.

Using Trends

We can use trends as sources for potential investment opportunities. If we can detect a worthwhile trend and then find investment types that best use that trend, we can then find specific investment opportunities that will best utilize that trend.

> Takeaway
>
> What trends are we looking for?
>
> Look for trends that are being driven by several factors/influences such as public demand, population growth, new regulations, economic structures, new

possibilities created by technology/innovation/knowledge, decreasing costs and building upon previous demands.

Look for more than one influence/factor which when they merge will magnify their individual effects and create an unstoppable force. Imagine what the world will be like in the future given the influence of all the factors pushing on the market. The more factors uniting to a similar direction the stronger the theme possibility. Constant reading about the trends (and themes as described below) and companies is necessary.

Look for why certain economical/ social/ industry/ markets outcomes are likely, what is changing and what is influencing possible outcomes to happen. Understand everything as a multi-dimensional space of factors effecting future outcomes.

Takeaway

Look for themes/trends that shift demand from an old way/product/service to a new way. Create a new demand where one didn't exist or themes that will change society, the economy, and people. These

> themes/trend should be inevitable and not fads as we will discuss later in the book.
>
> Look for trends that will have spinoff/cascade effects. These trends will impact some other element of society/economy causing it to change i.e. autonomous vehicles and the need to change car insurance.

Themes

Because trends can combine, we will define a theme to mean both an individual trend of interest and the merging of trends.

A theme is thus an abstracted representation of one or more trends. For example, there might be trends of eating less salt, processed foods and sugar but all are part of the overall theme of healthy eating. Similarly, the trend to high intensity physical exercise sessions is part of the overall theme of healthy living.

Trends can appear and disappear over time but themes tend to be longer term. For example, with healthy eating we have seen a number of trends appear such as low carbohydrate diets or the Mediterranean diet. Trends can last for quite a while but the theme of healthy eating seems relatively long term.

Summary

- Innovation, knowledge and technologies are combining in ways that are creating changes in society and economy that are unprecedented.
- We can look for specific themes such as those that will create a new demand as ones that might be investable.
- Themes tend to have associated investment opportunities.
- Themes are long term and align with a long-term investment horizon and thus create an investing potential for the average individual investor.

"We do not need a crystal ball to predict the future. We can have the gift of foresight though by understanding how cause and effect works."
Jeffrey Lehman

Chapter 6 Investable Themes

As mentioned in the previous chapter, investing in long term future-oriented themes particularly emerging ones, can be profitable and is also an area which large short/medium term investor typically don't focus on. We are in an era of almost unprecedented change brought about by the incredible convergences of technologies and knowledge as we can see in the figure below. In this chapter we list many of the changes occurring with a brief description. When reviewing the list consider the potential of each to have 1 or more of the following impacts:

1) Replace current ways of doing things.
2) Develop new markets or service new customers.
3) Create new business models including reducing costs, increasing customer revenue, saving time or doing different.

Consider the following:

By 1900	By 1945	Present day	When the Internet of Things is online
876000	219000	17520	12

Figure 2: Hours it takes to Double the Level of Human Information

3D printing

3D printing might provide the ability of the average individual to become a product producer and sell to other individuals similar to how YouTube become an outlet for creative individuals. Individuals might design a product and sell the design of it online for others to download and then use to print the product. 3D printing should also impact the manufacture of prototypes and replacement parts.

5G networks

5G networks will be implemented over the next few years enabling internet speeds of significant magnitude and providing the infrastructure for new remote services including the Internet of Things and autonomous vehicles.

Anti Aging

As a species we are living longer and healthier but we want to take that to the next level and add more years of healthy quality living to our lives as well as more years.

Artificial Intelligence

The ability to find patterns in data and then use them for enhanced data driven decision making will also enable devices to do work for us.

Autonomous Vehicles

Vehicles in hospitals, quarries, and on the roads that self drive will change ownership models and create mobility as a service.

Biotech

Technology related to improving the human condition including both mental, physical and mental ability is expensive to develop but the potential to change lives means that a market is there.

Blockchain

Blockchain technology can provide a trusted ledger of accounts and decentralize many industries including the financial, and organizational supply chains.

Cannabis

Cannabis has the potential in industrial, medical and recreational markets as both a market creation product and a replacer of existing products.

Cloud Computing

As computing becomes more complex, the need to scale organizations in a cost-effective way, along with increased focus on security and privacy would mean cloud computing is a viable solution.

Computing Visualization

Visualization of information for entertainment and decision making is important as we spend more time in front of the screen and need to understand the information we see.

Customer Relationship Management

Interacting with customers becomes more complex as organizations attempt to better anticipate their needs, particularly as we use self-service and e-commerce sites.

Data Analytics

Similar rationale to artificial intelligence, making sense of the massive data sets that technologies such as the Internet of Things will generate will the need for more automated tools.

Digitization of Business

Digital business not only reduce costs around printing, transporting and storing paper but we can measure digital processes to find better ways of doing activities.

E-commerce

Ecommerce is significantly impacting the retail industry as we move to delivery in hours (rather than days). As well, the technology is developing such that the average person can become a merchant. We are rewriting the commerce business model around products to create a more volume focused industry.

Edge Computing

With the internet connected to all types of devices, not all data has to be transmitted to a computer server for analysis. Some of the analysis will be done at the device level. Think of your toaster being smarter.

Educational Technology

The educational system is largely unchanged for the last century. Educational technology means individuals learning at their own pace when they need new knowledge. It means knowledge in small modules and the software guides the individual based on their learning needs.

Environmental Cleaning

Climate change is a significant challenge. Technology that can remove carbon from the air or toxins from the land/water and soil will be of value.

Extraction of Chemical Compounds

The products that we consume and use can have toxic by-products or have useful compounds or can be mixed with other chemicals in an organic mass which are not of use. Chemical extraction could help in medical and health related products.

Fintech

The world has been considering moving to a cashless digital economy for some years and there are benefits in creating frictionless payment systems in terms of reducing costs and tracking of money.

Gaming

E-sports and gaming is a significant entertainment area for people and the technology to lower equipment costs while increasing game value continues to improve.

Gig Economy

Using our time, expertise or assets we own to make income means software platforms need to bring people together for person to person transactions.

Health Technology

Everything related to understanding one's health and improving upon it aligns with the movement for better quality of life decisions.

Human/Computer Interface

Humans need faster, more intuitive ways to enact with computers including ways that we can better communicate preferably without direct hand contact. As we need to interact along a multitude of information types, the interface becomes more intense and we need to improve how we interact with computers.

Infrastructure

The need for moving, and storing physical objects including people, water, electricity as well as digital information streams will increase.

Internet of Things

It's estimated that we will have 10 sensors or internet enabled devices for every person on the planet within a few years including cars, stoplights and home appliances. This represents significant reworking in how we need to restructure our lives around data and the ability for devices to make decisions.

Information Technology Security

As we continue into the internet enabled future, including autonomous vehicles, it all requires secure data transmission, storage and access.

Logistics/Supply Chain Management

The movement of objects to people and locations including returns and disposal of objects will get more complex. This is of importance as we move in a more real time delivery world where transparency of object movement, environment impact and sourcing are more important.

Natural and Lab Based Foods

Health concerns are increasingly of concern to people. People want to know what they are eating and that their food is grown, stored and processed in the most humane way possible.

Open Data/Individual Data Ownership

With the data privacy violations we have seen over the last few years there is a sense that people should be able to control who has access to their data including derivatives of it. This suggests a change in who owns data. As well, thought is being given that data currently owned by large organizations such as financial institutions should be accessible by innovators to spark further innovations.

Open Source Software

Open source software is a mature industry and even used within proprietary software products. Open source business models have evolved to enable companies to make money from open source technology.

Plant Based Foods

Nutritional (healthy eating) guides are promoting the concept that humans should eat more plant-based foods and less meat. This aligns with environmentalists who are concerned with the amount of energy, water and space required to produce meat.

Purification of Water

Clean drinking water including cleaning it, transporting it and storing it will be of increasing concern as global warming increases and readily available water supplies shrink.

Quantum Computing

Quantum computing promises a breakthrough in the complexity of computing problems that can be solved. For example, providing better prediction algorithms for weather forecasting.

Real Estate

As the world migrates and intensification of cities continues, people need places to live and store products along with better business models to reduce costs.

Regulatory Compliance

As governments continue to focus on understanding monetary, trade agreement adherence and product flows, the need for transparency along the supply chain will increase. Along with more automated monitoring of regulatory compliances in other areas such as environmental issues, companies will want to reduce costs while ensuring no compliance gaps.

Renewal Energy

The cost of renewable energy is declining and as we move in the era of electrical vehicles and the Internet of Things, the amount of electricity needed is increasing.

Robots

Using machines to do physical and/or dangerous tasks has a wide range of applications from lowering the costs of manufacturing to performing medical surgery.

Social Media

Although this is a mature field, people still have the need to interact with others when separated by time and location.

Space

Space objects can be mined and advances in medicines obtained by utilizing technologies outside the earth's atmosphere. Costs for the space industry are decreasing making viable business models that were once only possible with large government programs.

Virtual/Augmented Reality

Interacting with information and other people using an augmented display holds potential in both business and consumer products such as shopping, entertainment and product repairs.

Wearable/Embedded Technologies

Wearable technologies provide the potential to monitor activity and free a person's need to interact with a device using their hands. Wearable technologies could also be the prelude to embedded technologies within the body.

Excluded Themes

- **Commodities** – These tend to have low profit margins and be cyclical. They often depend on the success of other sectors that use the commodities and thus can fluctuate. In addition, substitutes for commodities with other innovative materials is possible. Technological improvements tend to find ways to use less of the commodity, provide substitutes for it or drive the profit margin down. We don't include gold and silver in this category but will discuss them later in the book.
- **Oil/gas** – This industry could see a significant downturn as we move to renewable energy and away from carbon-based fuels. In addition, the supply (and thus the price) of the product is dependent on foreign political decisions which can suddenly and unexpectedly change. Renewable energy is at or near the cost of

carbon-based fuels making the oil/gas industry one on the decline.
- **Natural Resources** – Similar to commodities and oil/gas, natural resources tend to have low profit margins and be cyclical although the industry is attempting to modernize and drop the breakeven cost point of the product.
- **Crypto Currencies** – We are moving to a cashless digital society where crypto currency might be more regulated. It's not clear where this market is going. Currently, the market for crypto currencies seems more a home for speculators rather than investors.
- **Financial Institutions** – Financial institutions tend to grow with population and level of financial need in the population and thus are moving to more wealth management approaches. However, financial institutions are still largely dependent on interest rates which isn't something they set (usually a central government agency sets interest rates) and effects the entire industry's profits. Although its not clear that central banking setting of interest rates is fully reflected in the interest rates that banks charge their clients.
- **Pharmaceuticals** – Biotech and pharmaceuticals have the potential for long profitable product life cycles. However, anything health related for humans tends to have a high R&D cost, complex science, long proof of benefit/safety cycles through medical experiments and a high risk of failure.

Once we have our investable themes, we need to look for how to invest in them.

> Takeaway
>
> We increase our likelihood of choosing our investable themes by:
>
> Considering how individual themes might evolve.
>
> How individual trends might reinforce each other to become an unstoppable force.
>
> Consider what will happen next once a trend has matured. For example, once a new business model or innovation has changed society and the economy then what will happen next? It's thinking a few moves ahead that gives us the longest time horizon plan.

Examples

Let's consider three examples that illustrate the theme concept: Shopify, Canopy Growth and Microsoft.

Shopify

Shopify aligns with the e-commerce trend. Selling directly to the consumer has been a trend for several years. Manufacturers can sell directly to customers or through an online market place. Indeed, Amazon and eBay both provide an online market place where the seller could connect to the buyer. Other sites such as Craigslist and Kjjiji provide the capability for a person to sell a used item to another person. YouTube provides the ability for people to mass distribute their creative videos. In total, the aforementioned sites have help establish the e-commerce and online market place concept in people's buying behavior.

Amazon focuses on the customer and provides a market place for buyers and sellers. Shopify provides an online market place for merchants particularly the smaller merchant. Shopify provides a low risk, low learning curve opportunity for the average person to establish a business. On Shopify the average person can create a site to sell what they produce or even set up a drop shipping site to sell products that other companies produce.

If we look at the following stock price history of Shopify vs the Nasdaq 100, we get 4 take-aways.

The Nasdaq 100 has several technology company listings so it's a reasonable comparison.

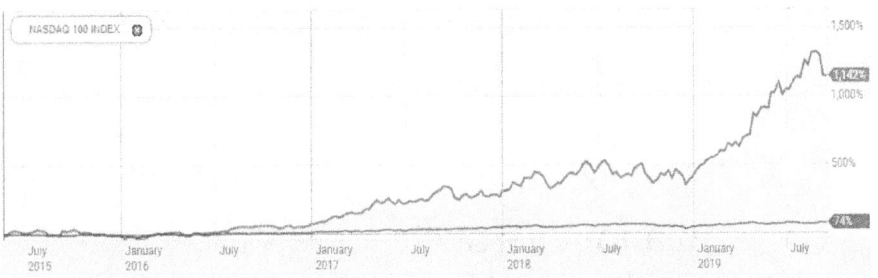

Figure 3: Shopify and the NASDAQ 100

Takeaway

Initially Shopify's stock was fairly flat after its public listing. It took awhile for it to deploy its capital that it acquired from the company's public stock market listing, to use.

We see volatility during the mid portion of the time line.

As the company started to demonstrate results it came into the broader investor market and its price rapidly increased with some volatility.

If we had bought it a few months after its public listing we wouldn't have seen much growth in the stock price until about 12 months or so.

Takeaway

> When would have been a good time to buy Shopify? Likely a few months after its initial public offering as the money deployed started to show results but before it became a widely sought-after stock.

Canopy Growth

Canopy Growth is in the cannabis industry which has several interesting factors. First cannabis is aligned with 3 potential markets: industrial, recreational, and medical. Which is a triple alignment into very different markets. The potential of the industrial and medical use is only estimated and not well understood. Recreational cannabis use is already a mature market, but one run by criminal organizations, so legal cannabis is replacing one source for another. That replacement possibility extends into tobacco and alcohol as cannabis products could take market share from those two industries. In addition, legal cannabis is an emerging industry and thus its entire infrastructure has to be established including the supply chain, financing and talent. In the following figure we compare the S&P 500 to Canopy Growth. We use the S&P 500 to represent companies that would be the alcohol and tobacco industries.

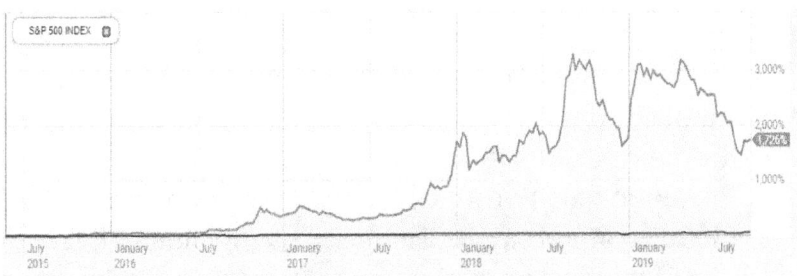

Figure 4: Canopy Growth and the S&P500

We see two major takeaways.

Takeaways

The volatility of the stock price would make holding the stock an emotionally draining situation. However, as we can see over time the return was overall still quite profitable. The volatility happened as the stock progressed from short term traders to retail investors to being held by large institution funds. In addition, as a new industry there was a much uncertainty around how that industry would shape out.

The legal cannabis industry was not established and thus had more volatility as its uncertainty swirled around each aspect of the industry's establishment including legality, regulation, quality, and internal processes.

Microsoft

Unlike the previous two examples, Microsoft is not a focused on one trend, instead there are several themes that its aligned with, such as artificial intelligence, Internet of Things, open source software, cloud computing, autonomous vehicles, IT security and digitation of businesses. Microsoft is a large well-established company and had a significant change in leadership and organizational culture change a few years ago with the company re-inventing its innovative spirit.

A large diverse company aligning with a theme might not have much of a significant impact but with Microsoft they aligned with many, such that much of their company was aligned with emerging themes in software. As we can see they have outpaced the broader NASDAQ 100 index. In addition, Microsoft pays approximately 1% dividend.

Takeaways

Larger companies can be worthwhile in a long-term emerging portfolio but the impact of the themes on the company should be significant.

As a crude metric, look to how many significant themes the company is aligned with to gain a sense of the company's potential. Its not a perfect metric as each theme differs in potential.

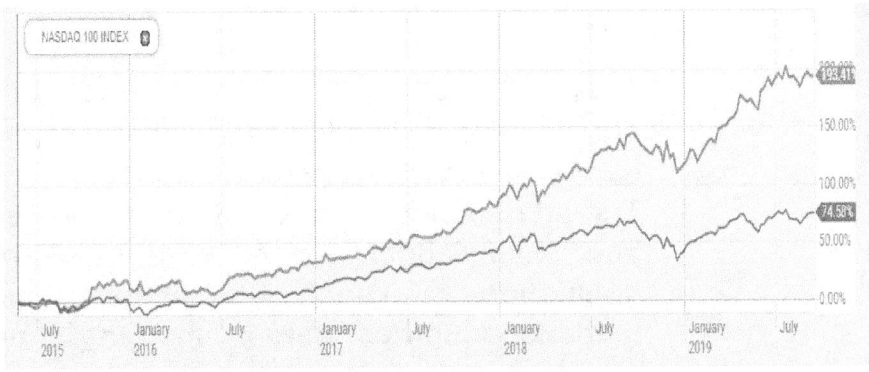

Figure 5: Microsoft Stock Price Compared to the Nasdaq 100

As we see with the Shopify, Canopy Growth and Microsoft examples, buying the stock early and then holding it over time, even through the volatility, paid off. It pays off more than holding the comparable index.

Summary

- Change in society, professions, industries, organizations and the economy is happening at an unprecedented rate.
- The intersection of innovations, technology and knowledge is causing a cross pollination such that new markets/industries are emerging, new business models are possible and untapped customer needs can be addressed or even created.
- It's at the intersection of trends that we can find long term investable themes.
- Our examples showed the return possible by taking a long-term view and holding an investment as it establishes itself, generates returns and becomes better known.

"The stock market is the story of cycles and of the human behavior that is responsible for overreactions in both directions." Seth Klarman

Chapter 7 Cycles

Economies, human psychology and society tend to move in broad cycles. Each cycle has differences in terms of its length, spark, and attributes but are similar in that a cycle of expansion will **cause** a cycle of contraction and vice versa. This broad pattern is generally repeated and thus can be anticipated and used as part of a long-time horizon investment strategy.

The key concept to note is that a cycle will tend to **cause** the inverse movement to happen (expansion/growth and then contraction/decline and then expansion/growth).

Extremes cause reversals because asset prices become too expensive or too cheap. As we move in one direction of a pendulum inevitability the pendulum will swing back. However, in the case of the economy, the long-term trend is upwards. Set backs happen but overall the direction of movement favors economic expansion.

The cycle drivers tend to be:

- capital availability (cheap financing such as low interest rates or too many investors all looking to invest somewhere).
- human psychology (which causes variation in the attributes of a cycle and extremes).
- the earnings of the asset.
- the status of the economy.

Cycles have beginnings, a middle and then the extreme point. Market greed/bull or market fear/bear are extremes. The details and timing and extent and people behavior of each cycle varies[5]. This variance means the broad pattern repeats but the unique attributes of a particular cycle can differ.

> Takeaway
>
> We don't need the ability to predict or listen to the financial or business media with their short-term unreliable predications. However, we can use cycles to generally anticipate the direction of the market and corresponding risk of a direction change.

---

[5] Do not assume each cycle will be exactly like a previous one other than it will start, have a middle and an end.

Cycles Lead to a Broad Timing Framework

We don't know the future but we don't need to because we can use the knowledge that cycles happen and the tendency/likelihood of what will happen depends on where we are in the cycle (beginning, middle, or extreme). There are two extreme positions: greed and fear. Greed is when investors are overconfident of the future earning and value of an asset type. A fear stage is usually when investors are afraid of the economic conditions or the particular asset class's value to earn future revenue.

We need to note how risk and potential return on the asset class align with the cycle stages.

Cycle Stages

1. Bottom of the cycle (fear): the market has experienced rapid stock price declines (bear market) and the economy is in a recession/depression or feared to be in one soon. Investors believe the economy can't improve, there are few sellers left i.e. low volume of selling in the market.
    - Therefore, the risk is **lowest**, potential future Return on Investment (ROI) is **highest** and the likelihood of a subsequent growth stage is **highest**.
2. Increasing stage: Investors believe economic improvement is happening, volume of stock buying increases.

3. Top of the cycle (greed): the market has experienced rapid stock price increases (bull market) and everyone is investing. In addition, the economy might be in full growth, investors think stock price increases will continue forever and volume of buying is slowing.
    - Therefore, the risk is **highest** and potential future (ROI) is **lowest**, because the likelihood of reversal to stock price decline is **highest.**
4. Decline of the cycle: this stage is a buying opportunity when stock prices are below their intrinsic value.

Why Does this Cycle Concept Work?

Consider the following figure. In the extreme greed/bull market, asset prices are above a reasonable value (also called intrinsic or fair market value) and thus investors will tend to sell the asset.

As extreme optimism prevails and unrestrained financing/investing occurs this results in unwise financing/investing, inflated prices, and thus the decline will eventually result.

The mid point of the cycle is rarely obtained but serves as an inversion point as the movement continues through the mid point.

In the fear/bear market, prices are below a reasonable value and thus the ROI potential is highest and people will eventually tend to buy the asset. As extreme pessimism prevails hesitant/restrained investing/financing occurs so only the best opportunities tend to get money.

> **Takeaway**
>
> The further the extreme the bigger the reversal tends to be.

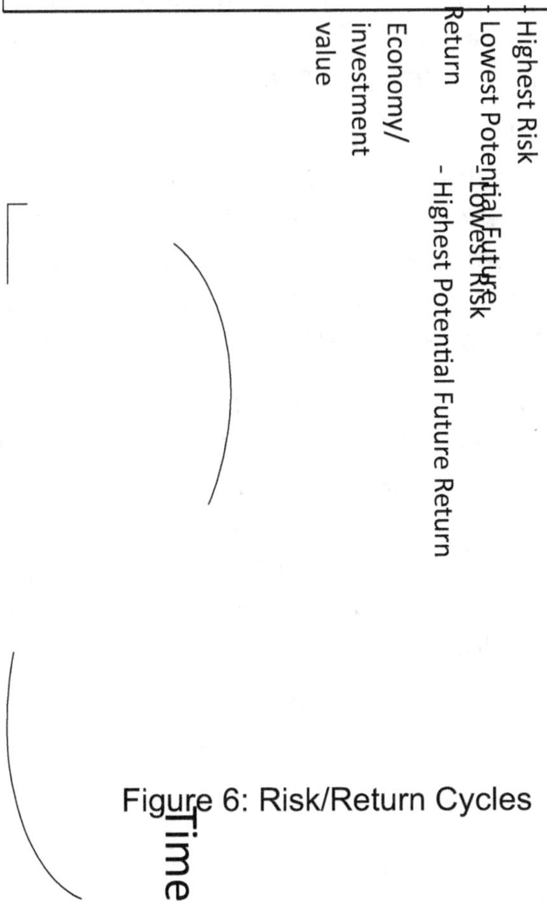

Figure 6: Risk/Return Cycles

Traditional Thinking on Cycle Stages

Traditionally when an asset has experienced rapid price increases some investors start buying because they believe the momentum will continue up and they don't want to miss out on the gain. So further upward gains are possible due to the late investors moving into the market. However, from a profit return point of view, the likelihood for further upward gains starts to diminish. Indeed, the likelihood for a downward move increases as the price of asset increases. Thus risk is actually higher when assets are overpriced.

Conversely when the cycle is at its bottom, some investors fear the market will continue down and sell. However, as the market continues down then assets become underpriced and the potential for stock price increases, aka return, actually increases. In addition, the risk of further price declines tends to decrease.

Note: We aren't necessarily speaking of a particular investment i.e. a value-based investing strategy that we discussed in an earlier chapter, where there is the potential for the value trap. Instead, we are discussing how an industry or society or the economy as a whole tends to move along the stages of a broad cycle.

> ### Recommendation 6
>
> At the extreme greed top of the cycle, move to prevent losses and/or start increasing your cash holdings to 5% or so. At the extreme bottom move to buy opportunities. In between the two, simply monitor.

Cycles are like Ocean Tides

When a market for an asset declines as seen in the prices for assets, we sometimes see panic ensue from the average individual investor and selling of assets occur. Perhaps the mass selling of assets is due to the notion that the money has exited the asset's market and may never return. Instead we should think of the situation similar to tides in an ocean. Occasionally the tide goes out in an ocean bay and we see bare ground perhaps sand or rock. The water hasn't evaporated or ceased to exist; it has gone somewhere else for a while. It will return and then fill the bay again with water.

Let's continue that analogy further. Often in areas with a tide we can see a high-water mark which is where the water reaches when the tide is in. Normally this water line will be obtained again when the tide returns. In a company stock we can consider the resistance price to be the high-water mark. A resistance price is a price point where the stock's price hasn't raised much above over recent history.

Some stock analysis sites will display the resistance line for a stock price. For other assets we can look at historical prices to get a sense of what is the current high-water market is for the asset. When the tide goes out, we can take advantage of it by exploring the ocean floor normally covered by water. Similarly with an asset, we can buy the asset at its low water mark.

We can look at historical prices to gain a sense of what the low water mark is, or for a stock we can use what is referred to as the support price. The support price is the lowest price that investors will pay for a stock in the current economic situation with the asset's currency income generating potential.

When the tides go out it's a good time to consider buying an asset. We might not know where the exact low tide mark is but it doesn't really matter because we know that we are below the high tide water line, so its all good.

Where are We?

As mentioned, understanding where we are in the cycle is an advantage that we can use. We don't need to understand precisely where we are, for example, at the peak of a cycle but just in general what cycle stage we are in.

Reading the business and financial news can give us an indication. The media tends to post both positive and negative articles about the state of the economy and market, and where its expected to go. Often the media will post positive and negative perspectives about the economy or an asset at the same time. A crude metric is not the whether the articles tend to have more negative or positive themes but whether an overwhelming sense of doom in the media is present. This might indicate that we are nearing the bottom of a cycle while an overwhelming sense of enthusiastic good tidings might indicate we are near the top of a cycle.

Another indicator is the CNN Fear and Greed index, see at:

https://money.cnn.com/data/fear-and-greed/

The index has 7 components to it. The index and its components are crude indicators. They can indicate short and long term down turns in the market. However, they aren't a reliable indicator of a recession or expansion as they will also indicate short term downturns without indicating what length of downturn is underway. As well, the indicators don't indicate the top or bottom of a cycle as a stock price downturn could be followed by an upturn and then a more severe downturn.

Two indicators of a recession have been the breadth/volume of stocks enjoying a price increase as seen in the McClellan Volume Summation Index and Stock Price Index Strength. For example, if the number of stocks going up exceeds the number going down, usually a recession isn't immediate. However, they are a crude indicator, if for example, i.e. investors are abandoning small company stocks and rushing to large well-known companies. Then the breadth is shrinking even if the overall market is increasing. It would be interesting to know what industries, regions and types of companies are seeing stock price decreases or increases and whether the concentration is moving to large well-known companies.

The Junk Bond and Safe Haven indicators are also interesting. They indicate whether investors in low value corporate bonds are requiring higher interest yields than safe bonds such as U.S. treasury bills and whether investors are moving to safe bonds. Typically, as investors become more concerned about the future of economy low quality bonds require a higher premium as investors gravitate to safer bonds, sometimes referred to as the credit spread.

In the following figure, we can see how seven different economic indicators were trending for the last major recessions. We can see how the majority of the indicators were aligned in a negative direction for the more severe recessions such as 2008-2009.

There is some argument that the economy has changed over the decades and once relatively reliable indicators don't have the significance they once did. For example, inflation and employment rates tended to be correlated but they may be decoupled due to the current structure of economy.

Start of Recession	Yield Curve	Inflation Trends	Job Creation	Credit Perform	ISM Mfg.	Earnings Quality	Housing Market
Nov-73	⬇	⬇	⬇	--	⬇	--	⬇
Jan-80	⬇	⬇	⬇	--	⬇	--	⬇
Jul-81	⬇	⬆	⬆	--	⬇	--	⬇
Jul-90	⬇	⬇	⬇	⬇	⬇	⬇	⬇
Mar-01	⬇	⬇	⬇	⬇	⬇	⬇	↔
Dec-07	⬇	⬇	↔	⬇	⬇	⬇	⬇
Present	⬇	⬆	⬆	⬆	↔	⬆	↔

Key: ⬇ Recessionary ⬆ Expansionary ↔ Neutral

Source: Standard & Poor's, Federal Reserve, BLS, National Statistical Agencies, NBER, ISM, Census Bureau, Haver Analytics®, Credit Suisse

Figure 7: Recession Dashboard

Summary

- We don't need to predict the future or listen to those that make such predictions.
- We can use the broad cycle approach to our advantage by tailoring our investment timing to where the economy and society is in the cycle along with what stage other investors think society and economy is in.
- Risk and return potential are linked to where we are in the cycle. At the bottom of the cycle is when we want to buy because risk is lowest and return likely highest. When the industry/economy, or in some situations an individual asset is at its highest then risk of a price decrease is actually at its highest and it might be time to sell the asset.
- There is no perfect indicator of where an economy, society or industry might be in its cycle but there are crude indicators which will give us a sense of where we are in the cycle.

"Risk comes from not knowing what you're doing." Warren Buffet

Chapter 8 Risk

Risk is often spoken of in conjunction with return on an investment. For example, seeking a potentially high return while undertaking a high risk might not seem prudent or advisable.

> Takeaway
>
> We can define risk as the potential of loss of some or all of our investment money.

Traditionally risk means identifying possible outcomes and their impact and likelihood of occurring.

Uncertainty is defined as unpredictable or uncontrollable events.

The two definitions clearly indicate that risk events have knowable attributes and have an element of control, i.e. mitigation techniques associated with them.

> **Takeaway**
>
> To invest in an opportunity primarily filled with uncertainty is more aligned with luck, speculating and gambling which we stated earlier in this book isn't aligned with the strategy discussed in this book.

To be clear, our risk and uncertainty definitions don't imply that investing in opportunities that are risky means we have perfect knowledge of what outcome and impact will occur. In addition, there might still be elements of uncertainty alongside the risk in an investment.

We can see risk associated with individual investments, the industry, state of the economy, society perspective, etc. There are many risk possibilities. Some are unexpected and referred to as a "Black Swan" since we didn't anticipate such an outcome occurring. Black swan events tend to have the biggest impact because they were unexpected.

Volatility as a Proxy for Risk

In the public stock market, we often see volatility presented as a proxy for risk. Indeed, in the Fear and Greed Index presented in the last chapter, there is a separate indicator for volatility.

The rational for using volatility for risk is that the stock market might be down when we need to sell our investment. This mainly holds significance for short/medium term investors who work on given time horizons. This is less true for long term investors who:

1) will not have sudden and unexpected need to sell.
2) will not have to sell at a predetermined date.

If an investor has a long-time horizon then an investment's short-term fluctuation in price are of lesser concern. Indeed, if the investor can decide to sell anytime during a long-time window then they can decide to sell when they decide the investment price is optimal, given that they have a sense of what is optimal.

Takeaway

Volatility shouldn't be considered a suitable proxy for risk when using a long-term investment horizon this is especially when the investor will not have to sell unexpectedly/suddenly and at a price they don't consider to be optimal.

The caveat is three-fold:

1) A volatile investment should still have a positive and consistent upward return over time.
2) Severe down turns in an investment's price need to have a higher price increase to return to the pre downturn price.
3) There is always risk associated with investments. Even investing in U.S. treasury bills is a risk, although very small, that the U.S. government won't honor its debt commitments.

Types of Risk

Cycle Risk – As we stated in the cycle chapter, risk tends to be lowest when the economic cycle/stock market has declined. Risk tends to be highest after rapid stock market increases.

Recommendation 7

Remove some risk by not selling at the cycle's bottom part but buying. As well, consider not buying at a cycle's high point but instead selling or holding the asset.

Caveat: With emerging industries and start-up companies its sometimes difficult to know where we are in the cycle since we don't have a history to examine. However, we can assume that rapid and recent increases/decreases in price are approaching or are at a cycle top/bottom. However, this top/bottom might be temporary and a result of actions taken by other investors. Indeed, a top might become a holding position until the asset provides proof of its long-term viability and then the asset continues to raise in price. Selling will be discussed again later in the book.

Correlation Risk – Assets, in general, have correlations with other assets or industries or the economy. For example, sector correlation might occur when consumer discretionary spending increases. Then manufacturing output increases as manufacturer's increase output to match increased demand. An obvious example is two car manufacturer's stocks could be correlated to what's happening in their industry. If car demand is down then holding stocks from multiple car manufacturers means all those stocks decline. Stocks are correlated to the stock market as a whole and thus if the entire stock market has a sense of euphoria, all stock prices might raise. Gold prices might act inversely to stock prices. A lowering of interest rates tends to precede corporate borrowing and thus expansions by corporations as they use cheaper money to expand their operation.

Takeaway

Consider how correlated the investments are to each other and the economy/market as a whole. Pick investments that focus on different industries, types of customers, business models, regions, etc. Technology isn't really an industry because the markets that technology sells to tend to differ.

Consider avoiding having more than 5% in a single investment or having multiple investments in the same customer market.

In general, when the stock market as a whole collapses then stocks tend to become correlated and all move down.

As the economy, society and industries change, correlation between assets changes. We assume correlations in different economic situations are valid for current economic situations.

Tool Tip: There are online stock correlation calculators such as:

Two stock Comparisons

https://www.marketinout.com/correlation/stock-calculator.php

https://www.buyupside.com/calculators/stockcorrelationinput.php

Multiple stock Comparisons

https://www.buyupside.com/calculators/stockcorrelationmatrixinput.php

https://www.portfoliovisualizer.com/asset-correlations

ETFs

https://www.portfoliovisualizer.com/asset-class-correlations

The above correlation tools look for correlations between the prices of the stock which is a proxy for understanding whether they are correlated with similar customers, regions, industries, etc. Correlation calculations are not a perfect substitute for understanding the business of the company along the lines of its customers, business models, regions etc. that were discussed in previous chapter.

Diversification vs Concentration – There are two schools of thought around diversification. Traditionally the main idea is to diversify your investments such that they don't have a correlation with each other so if one declines in valuation then perhaps another inversely correlated investment will increase.

However, there is also the thought that a too diverse portfolio begins to resemble the broad market of investment possibilities and thus reduces the purpose of building your own portfolio.

Indeed, Warren Buffet has advocated a concentrated portfolio.

> *"Wide diversification is only required when investors do not understand what they are doing." Warren Buffet*

While it might be higher risk, if we really have confidence in an investment then having fewer more concentrated investments could be worthwhile.

Takeaway

If we can't find opportunities that we have high confidence in, then don't invest.

In general, keep the number of investments smaller than 20-25. Some professional investors suggest keeping the number of stock market investments to less than 20. This could also result in higher portfolio returns as concentrated portfolios can do better than the market average. If the portfolio is more than 25 investments, then it might be just as good to buy an ETF.

Downside Risk – There is always the chance that an investment can reduce in price. Given the nature of cycles as discussed in the previous chapter, its worth considering selling some of an investment when its near the high point of the cycle. We could consider selling enough of the asset to gain the profits realized. This somewhat reduces risk since your profits have been taken out of the asset's total investment amount.

The advantage is that the profits can be used to build your cash position for other investments.

The disadvantage is that the asset might continue to do well. Particularly, the disadvantage is that: if the investment is a good investment then by selling some of it, we don't continue on its upside. Indeed, with start-ups, emerging industries, etc. there might still be plenty of runway for the asset to appreciate in value. We will be considering this advice again later in the book.

Summary

- Risk is the chance of losing money.
- Volatility is not a suitable measure of risk for the long-term investor.
- There are many types of risks and we can't protect from all risks.
- We can take steps to mitigate risk such as selling some of an investment to realize profits or buying when the economy is such that the asset is at a low price.
- The long-term investor can take advantage of volatility.
- Some of the risk mitigation measures also have the potential disadvantage of losing some of the upside profit of an investment.

"The individual investor should act consistently as an investor and not as a speculator. This means that he should be able to justify every purchase he makes and each price he pays by impersonal, objective reasoning that satisfies him that he is getting more than his money's worth for his purchase."
Benjamin Graham

Chapter 9 The Emotions of Investing

As discussed earlier in this book, we want a strategy to investing that is goal based and structured to provide decisions based on rational behaviour. Even with that structure its still difficult to invest without feeling the anxiety that results from asset price declines or the euphoria and satisfaction of profits. We can also feel the pressure to recklessly do better resulting from the envy of another person's investing success or the overcautious behaviour we exhibit from the market downturns that we witness impacting others or that impact us directly.

Its difficult to second guess our decisions and we do need to always seek to know what assumptions we have made and look to continuously validate those assumptions. We also need to recognize what emotional behaviours might be guiding our decision making.

By recognizing the emotional issues, then we can purposely attempt to manage them. The following section focuses on emotional based behaviors that we should recognize and be aware of their distortive ability on our cognitive thinking.

The following describe some cognitive mind traps that could cause one to make decisions based on emotions, and perhaps believe we are behaving rationally when we actually are triggered by emotional cues.

Narrative – Humans tend to like stories; indeed, our culture and professional lives might emphasize stories as a way to communicate guiding principles, especially if the story has relevancy and is familiar to our personal situation. With any asset there is usually a story as to why its in its current state and what its future potential is. We need to be keenly aware of each story that seems too familiar or attempts to draw connections with other irrelevant situations or has other attributes that make us draw false conclusions.

For example, an emerging investable theme could be developed around the need for animals and their suffering from anxiety. The story could draw parallels to human anxiety and suggest that an emerging investing theme is to use human based anxiety solutions for animals. Its familiar and for those with animals, is relevant. This narrative might draw a parallel to the percentage of the human population that uses a particular anxiety reduction solution and propose that the percentage of animals that will draw an equal benefit/usage will be similar. Thus, suggesting a significant market potential. However, humans have differences from animals. For example, we have a sense of the future and ability to understand why something is important.

Stories can close our thinking to patterns and alignments that are relevant and thus not suitable to draw conclusions from while providing a sense of false support for an idea which can't stand on its own.

Recency – We tend to overweight the significance of recent events compared to a longer-term pattern of events. We see this on the business and financial news media. For example, if a public company has a bad quarter perhaps due to a unique one-time event, then their stock price declines. Perhaps the event is an indicator that long-term potential and overall patterns have been disrupted. We also need to consider that recent events are not true indicators of the economy, society, companies, assets and industries. These have many influences on their performance.

At any one time, some of the influencers on an asset's future potential are in play but their effect might not be observable until sometime in the future. Some influencers react to others, such as managers and competitors reacting to news in their industry. When bad news happens, other aspects of the asset's environment i.e. people, might react to correct the situation. Thus news/events tend to trigger a reaction and so its not advisable to use recent news events to linearly extrapolate into the future. For example, a bad quarter indicates that future quarters will be bad. The recent news/event is an influencer on future events but not the only influence.

Recent events might not change the underlying rationale (assumptions) that we have for the asset but merely be a sideways movement or step backwards as the asset continues forward.

Availability – Information that we use to make decisions might be based on only readily available information which might be biased. For example, the media might focus on bad news or good news about the economy for periods of time. In addition, we might not have all the details about an asset to properly evaluate it. We then fixate on what is available rather than asking what type of information is missing and either searching for it or balancing our decision-making process. Given incomplete information we might not adjust our decision-making process accordingly instead mentally skip over the gaps.

Salience – This factor differentiates between the strength of a piece of data and its significance. For example, feeding chocolate to a dog can be fatal to the animal. This piece of data has a great negative strength against introducing a new type of chocolate food item into the market, but it's a not significant data point if the product is clearly intended for humans. As another example, we might become fixated on a data point that indicates that the sales in the U.S. of hula hoops is sharply declining but its not overly significant in indicating whether the U.S. is entering or already in a recession. We might also see a situation where the strength of a data point seems minor to the agriculture industry, such as bees not pollinating hobby gardens, but that could be significant (a highly weighted factor) because agriculture relies on pollination by bees and flower flies.

Relying on intuitive Reasoning – If two items are for sale and in total, they cost $1.10, and, one item is $1 more than the other, then what is the price of each? Some people will say one item is $1 and the other is .10 but thinking about it more carefully shows that correct answer is actually $1.05 for one item and .05 for the other. If we don't have the facts or algorithms or correct understanding, its tempting to substitute intuitive reasoning which can be significantly wrong.

Fear of Losses – Countless studies show people put more priority on not losing money in the short term then winning more money in the long term. This is a short-term mentality that sees the average investor selling shares when the market declines even though it's a bad long-term strategy and they have a long-time horizon.

Affect (herd mentality)– Investing in an asset can often mean taking a decision that others aren't aligned with, perhaps its because we are too early in the life cycle of the asset for others, perhaps they are using different data, algorithms, time horizons and goals. For whatever reason, there will be times that a contrarian approach or not investing with the herd seems to make sense and then we are proven wrong.

Wrong could be on the time horizon of the asset's potential, its return and other attributes such as its risk. Being wrong after we have gone against the investment decisions of others is significantly emotionally draining and should result in developing lessons learned for improvement. However, it can lead to a drag on our decision making as we start to doubt and hesitate.

We will be sometimes be wrong there are too many confounding variables, uncontrollable events, and unforeseen and unforeseeable outcomes to always be right.

Its thus tempting to invest with the crowd, so if it's wrong then it doesn't feel so bad because everyone else was wrong. Its painful to feel like we are the only one wrong but its not a valid reason to feel bad when wrong.

Confusing Judgement vs Luck - Sometimes our success or failures are just luck and not due to the reasoning we did. So, we need to be careful not to attribute success to our decision-making approach when it was just luck.

Takeaway

We need to use both successes and failures to re-examine our assumptions and decision-making approaches. We should be concerned if we don't know why we were wrong, and/or not able to correct our approach/strategy.

Point of Reference – the approach is to take a current event or price as the point of reference. If something is currently priced at $10 we will often hear analysts discuss whether where the price will go from there, perhaps stating that the asset is overpriced. Instead, one should look at how the company, its competitors, customers, etc. are changing and determine what seems to a reasonable future direction. Understanding where the company is attempting to go is important. However, using current prices vs historical prices as an analysis approach can be misleading.

Takeaway

The performance of your portfolio is more dependent on your emotional behaviours and resulting actions than it is on the behaviors of the assets in your portfolio. In other words, **emotional based decisions will diminish your returns and increase your risk**.

Focus on your goals, not your emotions.

Your portfolio is about your goals not your emotions.

Summary

- We should recognize the emotional aspects of investment decision making and by doing so attempt to manage them.
- Narrative, recency, availability, salience, intuitive thinking, affect and point of reference are attributes of decision making that are emotionally based.
- We need to continuously re-validate our decision-making approach.
- We will make incorrect decisions and need to use our structured strategy to help us manage the negative feelings that come from decisions that have negative outcomes.
- We also need to ensure that success in investing does not result in a euphoric feeling of invincibility.
- Investing is not a testament to our sense of being, it's an attempt to enhance our future.

"The stock market is designed to transfer money from the active to the patient." Warren Buffet

Part II

- Describe different asset types and strategic investment approaches using the long-term theme-based investment strategy.
- Describe an integrated strategy for the difference asset classes

"Have patience. Stocks don't go up immediately."
Walter Schloss

Chapter 10 Public Market Stocks

In this chapter we discuss implementing the long-time horizon theme-based investment strategy in public market stocks. We need to start with finding opportunities and evaluating them, and then address the risk, buy and sell considerations.

Finding Opportunities

There are many ways to find public stock market investment opportunities. Some investors will use filters or stock screens available on stock sites. They will search for company stocks that pass their particular criteria. The criteria might include debt, price/earnings ratio, return on equity and other metrics. After forming the short list, they need to undertake further research on the companies of the stocks on the filtered list to derive their watchlist[6].

---

[6] A watchlist is a list of stocks that an investor is interested in buying, usually the investor waits until a stock on the list becomes reasonably priced and then buys the stock.

While we aren't interested in "hot tip" stocks, we can attune ourselves to the financial and news media to hear of companies that pass our theme filter. Our theme filter is the first step then we can further evaluate the company. To find companies aligned with long term investable themes, we should read the specialized media that discusses innovations and new technologies along with media sources that discuss society and economic changes. Often in the specialized media we will see mention of companies focused on our investable themes.

We are looking for changes happening that are occurring over time and thus are trends, particularly the intersection of one or more trends. The intersections of trends or a series of changes can help re-enforce each other.

There are publications on most industries and topics, and many will also mention companies that align with our investable themes. We could note them in a document or spreadsheet. I suggest using a spreadsheet. List the themes and then the companies that align with the themes and then your rationale for the company. Listing the rationale is important. It is essentially your reason to buy and therefore your reason to sell. The rationale will inherently contain assumptions about the company's potential. If those assumptions prove to be invalid then it's a reason to consider selling the company.

Theme	Companies aligned with	What is happening with

	the theme	the company that suggests its best positioned to implement the theme. For example, management, products/services, business model, R&D, partnerships, etc.
Internet of things	XYZ	This company has patents that provide a barrier to entry around a critical part of moving data to cloud sites for analysis
Internet of things	ABC	Management has partnered with Amazon and Microsoft to be the preferred IoT data conduit.
Autonomous vehicles	XYZ	The hospital association policy document has standardized on a protocol and XYZ has the larger delivered market share of

		compliant vehicles.

Figure 8 Developing a Watchlist

> **Takeaway**
>
> Always know why you are buying a stock. The rationale should be future oriented.

Part of the rationale will be the alignment with the one or more investable themes. As we can see in the above figure Company XYZ is aligned with two themes making it a potentially more interesting company than ABC. In the following figure we see changes or trends happening in the ability the technology gives to do different, changing business models such as the way customers pay for a service and new knowledge perhaps due to a medical breakthrough. In the subsequent figure, we see society's perception of what is acceptable or desirable changing, as well as the state of the economy and government regulation. An example of such changes might be the cannabis industry in 2017-2020.

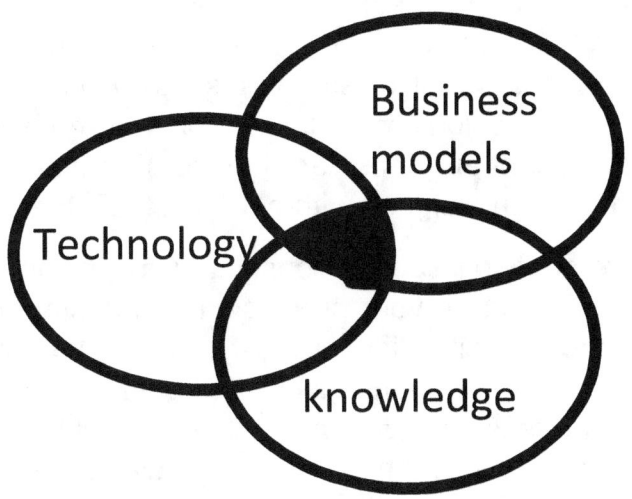

Figure 9: Changes/Trends Happening

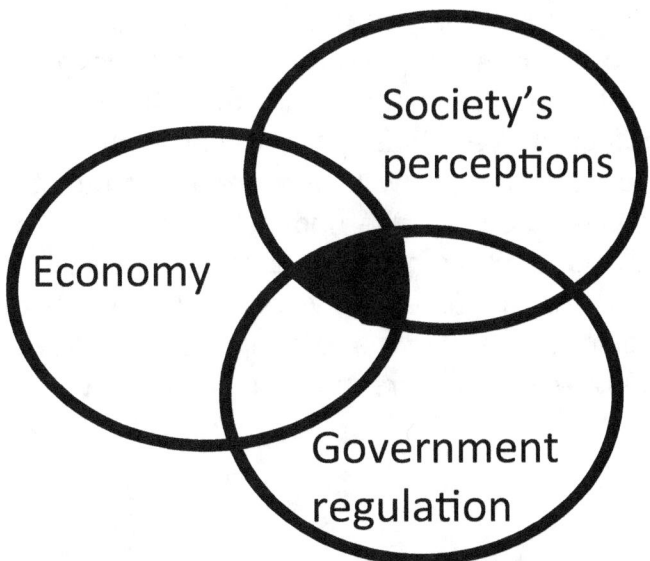

Figure 10: Changes/Trends

In additional to the public media as a source of ideas of companies aligned with our investable themes, you could also listen to discussions occurring in your profession or industry for the names of companies that are considered leaders, or innovators with a future and aligned with our investable themes.

There are two issues to consider with this approach of only focusing on your profession or industry news. First is the diversification issue. If you earn your living and return on investments from the same industry and/or profession you are not diversifying but concentrating. As mentioned in a previous chapter, that can be a positive given the opportunity presented, since you will understand it and will likely hear much about it through the normal industry chatter that you are part of. However, it also puts much of your future in one basket. Second, your familiarity, and presumably enjoyment, in the industry or profession can bias you. It can cause you to believe other people will also like the products and services offered by the industry i.e. you like the narrative and thus other people just like you will like it as well. We can immediately see the weakness of the preceding argument. It's perhaps better to view a company without a personal emotional attachment to it.

Creating Your Watchlist

There are two evaluation processes for creating your watchlist: quantitative and qualitative. Often with smaller or new companies we might not have the historical data that we need to do qualitative analysis. However, with both processes we want to look to the future for an indication of how the stock will do, with the understanding that the future is really a set of possibilities i.e. different scenarios, and, unknown and unknowable variables. Inherently any numerical based analysis tends to be historical, perhaps mixed with estimates of future results.

While there is support for the concept that a company recently doing well will continue to do well over the near-term future it's not so much the near-term future that we are interested in. Instead when devising our watchlist we are interested in the long-term potential.

Quantitative Assessment

In order to build a quantifiable rationale for placing a company on a watchlist we can review their numerical data if it's available. There are many metrics that can be used, successful investors will have the ones that they use and work for their strategy and data availability. It's difficult to say if there is one set of success metrics to use for all types of strategies. The importance of a metric can change given the economy or other factors. In this book, we look for metrics which are readily available on most stock investing sites and are relatively easy to use.

Typically, for quantifiable metrics to have value, we would want enough historical data to view how the company operates in different types of conditions. Conditions might be defined as different stages of a company's life cycle, economic conditions, selling into different region markets, management teams, etc. How many years/months of data that is available will vary by company and industry and this approach might not be suitable for emerging companies.

The following metrics attempt to understand the growth engine potential of the company[7].

> **Sales growth** tells us whether the company's growth theme is happening and can be measured by the rate of sales growth which should be increasing perhaps >20% per year.
>
> **Earnings per share** says whether the company is turning sales into profits and should be growing perhaps >20% per year[8]. This can be supplemented with the Price/Earnings ratio or Return on Equity ratio.
>
> **Free Cashflow**[9] provides the funding to continue growth. This is particularly interesting for companies where each additional customer doesn't mean a matching linear cost increase.

---

[7] Other interesting metrics include Return on Equity and dividend rate increases

[8] This needs to be considered carefully as some companies, such as those in emerging/growth industries or with significantly new business models might not initially fit these criteria.

[9] See notes

For example, online companies generate increasing amounts of cash with each new customer, particularly if their service is automated and self-serve.

> ### Takeaway
>
> Free cashflow is an interesting metric, as mentioned above. It's typically a significant metric for companies that provide Software as a Service (SaaS). Such companies, as they grow, don't linearly increase their costs with each new customer. Instead, their average cost per customer can decline. This means they have an increasing amount of cash that can be used to diversify the business.
>
> An example of that is Alphabet that can use its cash generated from its video site, browser and search engine, to diversify into cell phone operating systems and autonomous vehicles.
>
> When we see the potential for increasing free cashflow, its worth looking to see how it will be allocated. Will the money be used for short term goals that short-term investors favor such as share buybacks or will it be used to strengthen and diversity the company that long-term investors want.

> For example, Amazon has traditionally taken the long view which has meant their potential, as they use their cash to diversify, has increased.

Debt ratios indicate whether the company can withstand growth/economic issues. The current ratio should be >1. Debt can be used in interesting ways, for example, Brookfield Asset Management (BAM) when purchasing a company ensures that the debt of the purchased company is not attributed to BAM. This debt isolation approach means if the purchased company fails then the debt of the failed subsidiary isn't assumed by BAM.

Research and Development (R&D) indicates whether the company's growth potential is sustainable over the long term. Companies should have significant R&D, generate patents and have research in product/services outside their current main product line.

There is the argument that a company should focus only on what they are excel at and not diversify into unrelated areas. But what is unrelated? For example, Apple is good at building integrated products, innovation, and supply chain management. Apple's innovation has led them into developing an ecosystem of interrelated products and services. So sometimes seemingly unrelated product focuses might still use the core talents or capability or resources of the company.

Moat protects a company from competition, such as companies that have customers where switching costs are high, economies of scale, enjoy the network effect[10], have brands and patents or similar barriers against competition. We shouldn't consider traditional company attributes such as price, quality and functionality. These tend not to be sustainable barriers.

Qualitative Assessment

In addition to quantifiable metrics we should consider more subjective measures. In the following set of assessment categories, subjective judgement is required. This can be problematic if we aren't experienced enough or have the expertise to so. While experience can be gained over time, it is worth increasing our knowledge in these categories if needed.

---

[10] According to Wikipedia the network effect is the positive effect that an additional user of a good or service has on the value of that product to others. When a network effect is present, the value of a product or service increases according to the number of others using it. For example, the telephone has value when people you want to call also have a telephone.

Management Team – The management team's ability is critical to a company's ability to grow, evolve, make correct decisions and avoid bad decisions. Generally, look for a team that has had success in similar endeavours. Look for a team that might be well connected and are focused on the success of the company rather than their own success. Look for a team that can identify the issues and adapt their strategic and tactics. As an example, look to see what management does after a bad quarter or growth targets aren't being achieved.

Number of Theme Alignments – for our purpose, companies can be divided into three types.

> Large companies that do many things (lines of business or products/services) but only one of those things aligns with an investable theme. Such a company might not be significantly impacted by the theme and thus might not see significant growth due to the emerging theme. For example, airlines and autonomous vehicles.

> Pure play companies that are focused on one emerging theme. They tend to be smaller. For example, some renewable energy companies.

> Multiple theme companies - These are interesting. These are companies that are aligned with several emerging investable themes. In our watchlist we want to link the company to each theme. Such as technology companies.

Status of the Customer – The perception of the customer about the theme is important. In some cases, the customer is resistant to the theme such as cloning, in other situations the customer is readily prepared for the theme such as healthy eating. Situations where the customer has to be educated that a problem and a solution exist are less desirable than one where the customer is already aware of the problem or potential of a change occurring. If the customer isn't aware of the problem then it means the company will take longer to be successful (if they are) as the customer needs to be educated about the problem and types of solutions that will address the problem.

Conversely if the customer is well aware of the problem, that suggests that many companies will be working on their offering and thus the risk of choosing the wrong company increases.

Irresistible Force - It's the synergy of overlapping trends that creates an irresistible force of change. We want to look for a theme that has several forces pushing on it and where the combination of the forces creates a change/trend, which might be slowed, but can't be stopped. For example, an irresistible force of change might be temporarily slowed by an event or government regulation but can't be stopped. We see this in autonomous vehicles where early road accidents by autonomous vehicles were tragic but wouldn't stop the move to autonomous vehicles.

Portfolio

A portfolio should contain a diverse mix of stocks. Diversification does lower risk. for example, if an industry doesn't do well then a selection of stocks from the same industry won't do well.

There are many diversification strategies, for example, by having stocks from different industries, regions, whether they pay dividends and are of different company sizes. The aforementioned approaches are all viable and in use by investors. For example, some investors segment by industrial sector and then follow a strategy which sees a movement of investing between sectors depending on what state the economy is in. In an expansion stage, such an investor would focus on a different sector than during a recession. We discuss sectors and sector rotation in an appendix.

Let's explore the concept of diversification around certainty. Growth opportunities based on long term emerging themes aren't just applicable for technology companies. As we discussed earlier in the book, the convergence of innovations, technology and knowledge has created new business models, new industries and attracted different types of customers than we have previously seen. So many of the industries or sectors or regions can be experiencing more than just their traditional incremental growth but are transformational growth opportunities.

Let's divide the traditional sectors or industries along a certainty spectrum. Some industries or products are needed by people on a regular and frequent basis such as water, food and infrastructure. We can assign such industries a certainty factor in terms of their need by individuals. These sectors are well understood by customers and new approaches will be appreciated. These sectors might correspond with infrastructure, real estate and utilities and likely have dividends.

We define certainty to mean companies best representing a theme but there are unknowns around customer acceptance, the potential for customers to change their behaviour, replacing/creating new industries/markets, and support in terms of government regulation and economic structures.

Higher Certainty - Consider real estate. Everyone needs physical space to live and traditionally we have seen houses and apartments as the two main approaches to deliver physical space with the concept of ownership also segmenting the market. Some people rent and some own. Suppose a new approach that combined apartment living with house living appeared? Perhaps it would be similar to vertical farming where houses, including a yard, were stacked similar to a condominium but with a yard. The idea has both new elements to it but familiar concepts as well and the average person needs space. This might be a growth opportunity with higher certainty than the following: people are concerned about the environment. Suppose an inventor figured out a way than we could reduce the amount of carbon we exhale into the air with a breathing mask? The mask would trap carbon for later burial in approved underground storage sites. Likely this would have a higher uncertainty. While there is a theme around the environment, the average person would need to be educated (convinced) about the concept and its value, and change their life behaviours to adopt such a technology.

Lower Certainty - Companies such as Software as a Service (Saas) tend to have higher uncertainties when we are creating a new industry or replacing an existing one. These are typically smaller companies although its possible to find larger companies that are still undergoing strong growth rates. An example might be companies that are introducing new business models or new services to existing customers who don't realize they have such a need, for example, Apple and the first iPhone.

A portfolio should have a mix of uncertainty types with higher certainty companies that are aligned with growth themes perhaps in the area of education or real estate. As well, as lower certainty. As seen below, with some sample themes, we can group our portfolio along a spectrum of uncertainty to create a balance.

Real estate	Artificial Intelligence
Food	
Instructure	Block chain

Figure 11: Spectrum of Uncertainty

As shown below, our portfolio can be diverse by region, customer type, industry, business models, etc., and in addition, range along a certainty spectrum.

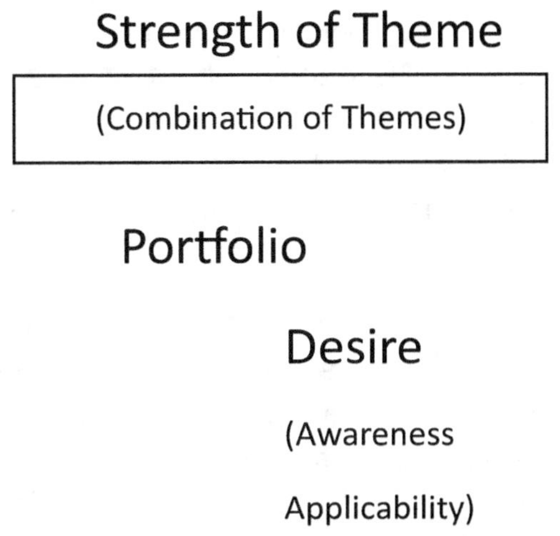

Strength of Theme

> (Combination of Themes)

Portfolio

Desire

(Awareness

Applicability)

Figure 12: Portfolio on a Certainty Spectrum

Takeaway

Previously we reviewed the concentrated vs non concentrated portfolio, and the suggestions from the investing community suggest that a portfolio doesn't need to be more than 20-25 investments.

Look for companies that benefit from alignment with more than one growth theme.

Company's Position in its Industry

Its worth noting every industry has a variety of companies in it. We can segment them along using a pipeline analogy. There are the companies that directly interact with the final consumer, those that produce components and those that supply raw materials.

Look for a position in an industry that is most profitable, e.g. is it the producer of the product or is the company that sells it to the consumer or the company that provides the raw materials. Typically, it's the company that has brand recognition with the consumer and intellectual property. As we can see in the figure below, the branded product might be recognized by the customer and thus have most of the profits.

| Raw materials | Components | Branded Product | Retailer | Consumer |

Figure 13: Industry Pipeline

Another possibility is a company that supplies an essential component to the product manufacturer. That component might be based on unique, irreplaceable intellectual property. As we see in the following diagram, a component is critical to several companies, for example, a computer chip manufacturer sells their chips to computer companies, cell phone companies, and even automobile manufacturers.

```
                    Branded Product        Consumer

    Component       Branded Product        Consumer

                    Branded Product        Consumer
```

Figure 14: Core Company in an Industry Pipeline

Allocations

How much to hold in each investment? As we have noted that can vary depending on whether you have high confidence in a concentrated set of companies or perhaps with incomplete information and/or less certainty you hold a wider dispersal.

> **Takeaway**
>
> Typically hold 5% of your portfolio in cash for opportunistic events.

Volatility and Emerging Themes

Emerging themes might be best realized with smaller companies. This approach gives us an advantage to buy early but we might need to hold the stock for quite awhile until the company matures. Once the big investors invest then potential ROI decreases. Day traders/speculators do buy smaller company stock, thus smaller companies can be more volatile until they have grown enough to attract bigger investments. Pure play companies are focused on one product line and thus when the theme comes to fruition their growth can be more significant than large companies that do many types of product lines.

We can then map the volatility of a company along its life cycle as seen in the following figure. The company might start on a junior stock exchange and be traded by day traders and short-term investors who are looking to make money on volatility, and will sell when the news is negative. Later the stock might move to a more senior stock exchange where it captures the attention of more retail investors and more importantly large institutional funds. This will tend to stabilize the stock price, particularly if it gets included on an ETF based on an index description. If the stock becomes the industry favored stock it could become the go-to stock for the industry, similar to the way Apple and Amazon represent their industries.

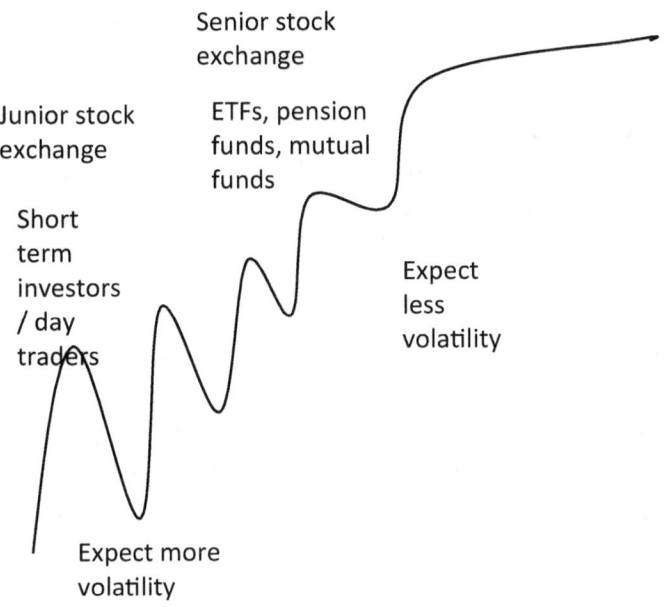

Figure 15: Volatility and a Stock's Life Cycle

Winner and Loser Stocks

Smart investing decisions can still lose and bad decisions can win.

Much of investing outcomes are outside of our control, so investing isn't so much about picking winners, its also about avoiding loser investments and being protected from significant declines.

Consistency is a metric of success in a portfolio, its not just the gains, but the avoidance of loss. If you decide not to do an investment and subsequently that investment doesn't do well then review your decision to gain an insight as what decision points were correct.

Buy/Sell

Its not a good idea to attempt to time the market but we can anticipate worthwhile time intervals based on the cycle concept we discussed earlier.

In general, don't look at your stocks every day. It takes time for management to implement their strategy. Instead, evaluate a company as to whether the management team is meeting its objectives and will continue to do so. For setbacks, consider whether the management team will be able to react and adjust its approach.

Buy when the economy is low or the stock market is in a bear market or the stock price is under its intrinsic value[11]. Invest when investor stock markets are scared and recently sold off, and, thus the odds are in your favour. Start buying when stock price is below its intrinsic value (fair value), such as 5% below. The lower it is below its intrinsic value then the more protection from further declines[12]. In other words, as the price declines there might be an initial

---
[11] See Notes section.
[12] Error zone – buying at a lower price helps protect us from the unknowable future and possible negative outcomes.

spark of selling as automated sell triggers are activated but as those complete, there should be a natural support price start to develop and the risk of further selling decreases. This assumes that the company doesn't have something fundamentally wrong with it.

Don't attempt to time the bottom price. Use part of your 5% cash reserves to buy and if the price goes down then buy more, assuming that the company isn't permanently in a sell off. Consider investing when a good company has a one-time bad quarter or issue that short-term investors don't like and thus sell.

Sell (or take profits) when extreme greed or the stock price is over valued. Take profit when investors are euphoric and thus the odds are against further increases and the risk is highest. Start considering to sell when intrinsic stock value is lower than current stock price[13]. Calculate profits gained from stock and sell at least enough stock to obtain the profits.

This needs to be considered against the long-term value of holding the stock, I am not suggesting repeated buying and selling of stock, that is potentially a money losing approach. Instead, consider selling some of the stock when it appears to have reached a plateau and likely to decline over a long duration. This selling to realize profits means adding to your cash position to held for the next stock purchase.

---

[13] This needs to be carefully considered as some companies, such as those in emerging/growth industries or with significantly new business models might naturally be higher priced than their intrinsic value.

Selling/Re-balancing

Generally, follow a buy and hold strategy but consider selling enough of a stock to obtain profits when its price has undergone a rapid increase.

Also consider selling when:

- A theme has matured.
- The company is declining with little hope for a turn-around.
- Sell if the company is implicated in falsifying their financial statements.
- When the cycle appears to have reached its peak.

In other words, sell when the reason you bought the stock is not longer valid.

Stop Order Strategies

This book advocates a long-time horizon investing and short-term volatility isn't really a concern. There is a way to automatically set a sell trigger on your stocks called a stop order. A stop order will trigger a sell order for the stock associated with it once a predetermined price has been obtained. Stop orders can have applicable dates or even just be valid for 1 day.

I want to briefly describe a trailing-stop order. The stop price trails the price of the stock as it moves higher. The stop price essentially self-adjusts and remains below the market price by the number of points or the percentage that you specify, as long as the stock is moving higher. Once the stock begins to move lower, the stop price freezes at the highest level it reaches.

In other words, the stop price can move higher indefinitely, but the stop price trigger can never move lower. If the stock falls enough to reach the stop price, the order is triggered and sent to the marketplace. The primary benefit of a trailing-stop order versus a regular stop order is that it doesn't have to be canceled and re-entered as the price of the stock increases. As mentioned above, this order is held until the stop price (trigger) is reached.

Stop orders should be used with caution. Often emerging industries and small companies are volatile and can experience sudden price changes, significant price declines followed by significant price increases. This volatility could trigger unnecessary selling and then re-buying incurring costs. While stop orders can give downside protection and thus some risk mitigation they might be counterproductive with a long-term strategy. So automatic sell order (triggers) should be used carefully.

Risk vs Return Over Time

In chapter 16 on bonds, I provide an analysis of risk vs return vs the investor time horizon for bonds vs stocks.

Notes:

1. A **bear market** is when stock prices fall and the overall view of the market is pessimistic. As prices begin to fall investors and traders begin to panic. This causes increased selling, which in turn, makes prices drop even lower. The beginning of a bear market is defined as at least a 20% drop over a two-month period. It can be a buying opportunity.
2. The **bull market** is when stock prices are rising and expected to continue. The outlook on the economy is strong and traders are excited about the future. When unemployment is low and the GDP is strong companies see a rise in profits. The optimism this causes is attractive to traders. They come in and continue to push prices up. It can signal time to sell enough stock to obtain profits.
3. A **bubble** is when people believe there is no or little risk and thus any high price is justified because there is no risk.
4. **Intrinsic (fair) value** is the perceived or calculated value of a company, including tangible and intangible factors, using fundamental analysis. The discounted cash flow (DCF) model is one commonly used valuation method. An intrinsic value/fair market value of a stock is provided by Morningstar which some online investing sites provide. As a widely used valuation it also will thus helps

form the psychological mindset of typical investors.

5. **Risk** is typically measured by the diversity or the extent that stocks in a portfolio are non correlated. Diversified stocks are those that react differently to a given market condition and aren't dependent on another stock's movement. Volatility as a risk measure is only important if one must sell at a given time and needs a given ROI.

> Otherwise, risk is about loss and can be measured by the uncertainty of potential range of loss and gain on an investment. Overpaying of a stock's intrinsic value is higher risk and potentially low return. Underpaying the intrinsic value is paying less than a stock's intrinsic value and thus achieving lower risk of loss and higher potential return. Overpaying for a stock means higher risk. When stocks are significantly overpriced then risk is highest.

A conventional way to measure risk is with the Sharpe ratio which measures the amount of risk undertaken compared to historical returns. A high Sharpe ratio is good when compared to similar portfolios or funds with lower returns. Adding non correlation investments to a portfolio can reduce risk. Variants of the ratio include the Treynor and Sortino ratios. However, an accurate measure of risk is unknowable only ways to reduce obvious risks.

6. The **beta** coefficient is a measure of the volatility, or systematic risk, of an individual stock in comparison to the unsystematic risk of the entire market.

7. **Recession** - Investors sometimes look at the difference between the 2- or 3-year US treasury bond rate and the 10-year rate to indicate whether a recession will occur. When its inverted i.e. short-term rates are higher than long term rates, a recession could occur over the next several months. An open question is whether the inverted yield curve predicts recessions or does federal government monetary policy? In other words, if the yield curve inverts government might move to stimulate the economy thus as the yield curve worsens then credit availability might increase simulating the economy.
8. **Free Cashflow** - cash a company retains after cash outflows to support operations and maintain its capital assets.
9. **Moat** - Advantage a company has over its competitors which allows it to protect its market share and profitability. It is often an advantage

that is difficult to mimic or duplicate (brand identity, patents) and thus creates an effective barrier against competition from other firms.
10. **Market/economic Forecasts and Analyst Recommendations** are essentially useless but they can influence the general thinking of investors and thus the movement along a cycle.

Company Valuation Indicators

1. **PEG** A lower PEG ratio is "better" (cheaper) and a higher ratio is "worse" (expensive). The PEG ratio of 1 is sometimes said to represent a fair trade-off between the values of cost and the values of growth, indicating that a stock is reasonably valued given the expected growth. A crude analysis suggests that companies with PEG values between 0 and 1 may provide higher returns.

   The Computer/Software industry currently had an average PEG ratio of 2.12 as of Spring 2019.

2. **Short Ratio** is the number of sellers hoping that a stock price will decline. A high short ratio is considered a bearish signal, while a low ratio is thought to be bullish.

3. **Stock Price/Earnings Ratio** If the forward P/E ratio is lower than the current P/E ratio, it means analysts are expecting earnings to increase; if the forward P/E is higher than the current P/E ratio, analysts expect a decrease in earnings.

4. **P/E/G** for growth companies divide the P/E ratio by the company's rate of earnings growth over the last three years. A desirable ratio <1.

Information Sites

Below we have listed sites to gain a sense of:

1. The fear and greed status of investors,
2. The state of the economy by looking at the bond market and seeing which debt financing is too available or not, and,
3. The stock market's historical profitability vs the current level of profitability. A above average profitability is a bull market.

Fear and Greed Status

The fear and greed status of the market can be seen at:

https://money.cnn.com/data/fear-and-greed/

State of the Economy

The following sites provide a measure of money availability. Typically, the yield spread is narrow in a bull market and wide in a bear:

https://ycharts.com/indicators/210_year_treasury_yield_spread

The long-term average of 0.95%.

Also gain a sense of debt (credit availability), at:

https://www.bloomberg.com/markets/rates-bonds

Price/Earnings Ratio

P/E historical comparison

S&P 500 historical ROI tends to be 10% or adjusted for inflation 7%.

Current S&P 500 ROI

current
https://ycharts.com/indicators/sandp_500_total_return_annual

https://ycharts.com/indicators/sp_500_monthly_return

https://quicktake.morningstar.com/index/IndexCharts.aspx?Symbol=SPX

https://www.investing.com/indices/us-spx-500-historical-data

Summary

- Look for company that will do well over time.
- Look for companies that match the unfolding trends in society or the economy.
- Always know why you are buying a stock and what changes will cause you to sell the stock.
- Look for a balance of stock types in terms of their certainty of earnings over the future term.
- Track a company on a watchlist, before considering to buy it to understand how its business model will do over time.
- Evaluate the company on both qualifiable and quantifiable measures.
- Practice with a watchlist to understand how the market moves.

"The key is in not spending time, but in investing it." Stephen Covey

Chapter 11 Options Trading

Options trading is a viable strategy to add an income stream to your stock portfolio and provide an approach, to a limited extent, that will reduce risk around a possible decline of a stock's price. As well, options can be part of your stock buy and sell strategy.

We include options trading in a long-term investing approach for its potential to:

- Reduce risk.
- It can be repeated to thus form a long-term approach.
- Take advantage of short-term investor's approach.
- Reduce the cost of purchasing or increase the return of selling a stock.
- Gain some more income when buying or selling a stock.

A stream of income resulting from an option strategy on a particular stock lowers the price you paid to acquire the stock. Assume that you bought a stock for $10 and with options trading you earn an income of $1 for that stock, then the cost of the stock is now $9. The income stream from an options strategy inherently has given you a way to somewhat reduce risk since the price of the stock can decline to $9 and you are still at break even.

In this chapter we discuss a simple Call and Put option approach to reducing risk by earning money on your stocks.

The Call and Put option as a basic unit of transaction can be used in a myriad of ways to create many possible strategies. Some of the strategies are high risk and we do not recommend them. Indeed, some option strategies could involve the potential for infinite loss.

Other investors might use options trading for complex strategies. They tend to be short term investors, particularly since options have an expiry date. Indeed, some traders only trade in options and aren't interested in acquiring the associated (underlying) stock. Thus, their short time horizon approach can work to our advantage. We will provide a summary of some of these strategies in this chapter.

You should learn what are Calls and Puts and their inherent risks before using them. There are so many useful sources of information that I wouldn't repeat the same information here. However, you should know at least the following concepts.

Concepts

Call options are agreements/contracts that give the option buyer the right, but not the obligation, to buy a stock. This is usually done when one anticipates an increase in price of the underlying stock.

Put option is a stock market contract which gives the owner of a put the right, but not the obligation, to sell an asset, at a specified price, by a predetermined date to a given party. This is usually done when one anticipates a decline in price of the underlying stock.

Options Contract – A single contract for options consists of 100 shares of a stock. In other words, you are agreeing to sell or buy 100 shares of the company per contract that the options are associated with.

Expiry date – Options have a start date and an expiry date. Trading and the option's value occur within those dates. An option's duration is typically measured in a few months. Upon expiry the options contract has no further value or commitments.

Strike Price – Is the price that the options contract is typically executed at. For example, if the current price is $100 then a strike price will be at and around that price. For example, there might be a strike price option at $110.

In the money is when the stock price is aligned with the strike price so that buyer of the option will want to execute it i.e. the option has a positive value.

Most online stock investment sites have an options page for stocks with complete details of current options, prices, durations and other data.

You need to understand the information on the options page. We wouldn't discuss the options concept and associated information in this book.

Takeaway

The starting point for an options strategy is the following rule:

You shouldn't buy a stock just for the purpose of options trading. Do your analysis on the stock and if it happens that you will buy at least 100 shares of the stock then consider options trading strategies.

The following two options strategy use either the Call or Put option.

Selling Covered Call Options

Assume you own at least 100 shares of stock. In other words, it's a Covered Call i.e. you own the associated (underlying) stock. Selling call options without owning the associated stock is risky and it is not recommended it and is referred to as a "naked call".

The selling part is a critical decision.

If you sell a covered call option the buyer could execute the option contract and buy your shares at the strike price, if you have decided that you don't mind selling the stock. Perhaps you have more shares then you deem to need or the future of the stock seems to be stuck in neutral for quite a while. In other words, you should have a valid reason why selling part or all of your shares for the underlying stock is acceptable.

Earning revenue from selling a call option works well if it appears the stock is stuck in a trading range and we believe that it wouldn't increase in value for some time. If you do have to sell the stock because the option was executed (called), you can decide whether to buy more of it or not. This stuck in neutral stage might happen in an emerging market where the management team needs time to implement their strategy so significant upward movements in the stock price are sometime in the future. Another situation might be that you figure that the stock price will slowly move up over the next time period associated with the option's expiry date but won't exceed the strike price.

If the option is executed then you have to sell at the strike price but you keep the profit gain resulting from the stock price increasing to the strike price and the money from the sale of the option. Obviously, you don't get any part of the further increase in the stock price profits after the sell transaction. You would also keep any dividends declared before the sale of the stock to the call option buyer, given that the date of record of who owns the stock precedes the sale date.

> Takeaway
>
> An interesting time to initiate a sell option is just after the underlying stock's quarterly earnings report. The earnings report might cause a change in the stock price and you want the impact of the earnings quarter report to settle before you sell a covered call option.
>
> As well, an option duration that includes a dividend date might trigger a call just before the dividend date.

Takeaway

When the stock is at a high point and doesn't appear to have significant upward momentum over the foreseeable future, it would be a good time to consider selling a covered call option.

If your stock has lost money for you i.e. the price has declined after you bought the stock, then it might not be time to sell covered call options. As a gain in the stock price could trigger the call and if you are still in a loss position with the stock then a paper loss becomes a permanent loss which might not offset the income from selling covered calls.

You can reassess your open call options as the price of the stock changes as to whether you it would be better to close the open call rather than have it called by the buyer. A calculation of the cost of closing the option vs the profit of keeping the shares and selling them your self will help indicate whether its worth closing the call. You can close the option with a "buy to close" trade.

> **Takeaway**
>
> In some cases, its worthwhile to close the option when the stock price has further declined. The call option will also have reduced in value meaning profit will be made between the open and close trade, as some stocks can have a significant rebound when they have been oversold.

As I discussed earlier in the book, the market tends to move in cycles. You want to sell a covered call option near the top of a cycle and above the resistance point so that the likelihood is that momentum will be down. This is not great for the underlying stock that you own but you will mitigate that downturn underlying stock price movement with the profit of the covered call option sale.

> **Takeaway**
>
> If you own more than 200 shares and want to keep some of the stock but are comfortable with selling some of your shares, one approach is to not sell options contracts for all your shares. For example, sell a covered call option on ½ or so, this way if the share price continues to raise beyond the strike price then you still have some of the stock.

In brief, the selling of covered call options works well when the stock price is **stable** or might decline and we want to have some downside protection for a stock price decline.

In Summary:

1) Ensure you have at least 100 shares of the stock.
2) Sell **covered call** options with strike price significantly higher than current price.
3) Works better for stable price stock or not expected to increase, such as when at 52-week high point, over the stock's resistance point or fear/greed in market is high.
4) Works better on stock with dividends.
5) Ensure that you are willing to sell the stock if the call option is executed.

The strike price that you sell the covered call option can vary depending on your sense of how the stock price's stock might move over the duration of the options. For example, a volatile stock could have quite a range of movement in the duration of the option thus a strike price mind needs to be high.

> **Takeaway**
>
> If you have a preference to keep the stock but don't mind selling, then choose a strike price high above the current stock price.
>
> If you are more inclined to sell then use a strike price higher than the current stock price but closer to it.

There are many strike prices and durations. Different combinations have different option prices. It's tempting to do the most profitable but that increases the chance that the strike price will be obtained and you have to sell the stock linked to the covered call option.

If your preference is to keep the stock then do a high strike price, make the money from selling the covered call option but don't be greedy. You can calculate the % that the stock would have to increase to obtain the strike price and then look at the stock's traditional volatility to gain a sense of whether the strike price could reasonably be obtained during the duration of the option.

Keep in the mind: If the strike price is $110 and the covered call option contract buyer paid $2 per share then likely they won't execute the call option until the stock price obtains $112. At $112 the covered call purchaser is breaking even and is interested in the increase in the stock price at that point onward.

If the stock price is approaching the strike price and you decide you would prefer to keep the stock, you could sell to close the option; it means taking a profit loss on the option trade.

Covered Call Option Risk

The risk associated with selling a covered call option is that if the strike price is obtained and we have to sell the stock, then we lose out on any further price increases in the underlying stock price which is referred to as an opportunity loss. That is why I suggest the strategy of only selling options on part of your stock and choosing a high strike price.

Never sell more call options that you have stock – that's a naked call option which is too risky.

Selling Covered Put Options

When selling a covered call option, we **own** the stock and don't mind selling it.

With a put option we **want to own** a stock but **don't currently own** it and we **have the money** to buy the stock.

A put option gives someone the right to sell us a stock when the price declines to the strike price. A short-term investor might buy a put option to give them some downside protection for the situation when the stock price declines within their time horizon of selling it. If the price declines below the strike price then the put option purchaser can execute the put option to sell the stock to you.

From our perspective, we have decided to own the stock over the long term and thus are happy to buy it when it declines in price. The stock price might decline further than the strike price, so we should be confident in the company that a price decease wouldn't be permanent.

If we have decided to own the stock then selling a **covered** put option at a lower strike is a viable way to acquire the stock at a lower price.

In Summary:

If we **want to own** a stock, then consider selling a covered put option

1) **Ensure** you have money to buy stock. *We don't do "naked put options".*
2) Be **confident** that you think the stock price might decrease.
3) **Sell covered put options** with a strike price below the current price.
4) The strike price should be within range of the stock's normal volatility or support price such that there is a reasonable expectation that the strike price will be obtained.

Don't be greedy. Its possible that a price decline could fall below your strike price and you could have bought it at a lower price. It's impossible to predict with accuracy the bottom of a stock price so be happy if you bought the stock at a price below its normal price as the following example illustrates.

Assume that the stock price is $100 and you sell a covered put option for $2 with a strike price of $96. If the stock price declines then you will be purchasing the stock at $96 − $2 collected from selling the put option, which means you are actually buying the stock for $94. If the stock price continues to fall to $94, you are still breaking even.

In some tax jurisdictions that allow tax free investment accounts, put options are NOT allowed within the tax-free account. They are generally allowed in taxable investment accounts. You need to check on your tax judication's regulations.

Risk of Selling Put Options

If the strike price is obtained and we are forced to pay the stock and the stock continues down in price, there is the risk that the stock decline is permanent. For example, assume a scandal hits the company because it is caught doing illegal activities and government moves to halt the company's activities. Then the price decline could be permanent, even move to zero.

However, if we had purchased the stock without selling a put option, i.e. we own the stock, we would still be in a similar situation. If in both situations we took no further mitigating actions to halt our ownership of a stock headed to zero then in both situations (selling a put option or buying the stock without a put option) the risk is similar.

We should have done our due diligence of the company and be confident that a price decline wouldn't impact our long-term expectations with that company.

Another risk is that the strike price is not obtained within the option's duration. Instead the stock price increases, the option expires and then we still want to buy the stock but its now at a higher price. Assume that the stock price is $100 and we sell a put option at a strike price of $95 for $2. If instead of declining to $95 where we would consider executing the option, the price raises to $105. We then decide to buy the stock at $105. We have gained $2 from selling the put option so are purchasing the stock at $105-$2 = $103 is what the stock costs us rather than $100 which is what we could have purchased the stock for if we didn't do the selling put option contract strategy.

As with the covered call, the risk of opportunity cost or loss can happen if the stock's price moves in a direction that doesn't work with our options strategy.

Takeaway

Always ensure you have the money to buy the stock at the strike price.

Never do a "naked put" which is when you don't have the money to buy the stock. If the put purchaser executes the put option then you would have to find the money quickly.

Repeated Selling Options

Both the put and sell options expire over time at a predetermined date. For selling the covered call options, you can analyze the stock's situation again (after the option has expired) and sell another covered call option. This process can be repeated, each time you are inherently lowering the acquisition cost of the underlying stock that you bought. You could continue to repeatedly sell covered call options (after each has expired) even lowering the breakeven point to where the risk of the stock going below your breakeven point is greatly diminished.

For the covered put option, you are unlikely to continuously repeat this strategy when attempting to buy a stock. For example, if the underlying stock continues to raise in value, you need to consider abandoning a continuous pursuit of the underlying stock using a put option and just move to buy the stock.

Other Option Strategies

As mentioned earlier while put and call options are simple mechanisms they can be used in a variety of ways. For example, some investors make a money just selling options and not buying the stock. This strategy of only owning options is not aligned with our long-term investment strategy, however, its worth understanding why other short-term investors might buy our covered options. Understanding how short-term investors use options helps our understanding as to why they would buy our covered options.

Short Term Options Strategy 1

Before discussing the strategy, we need to understand the concept of "delta" as it applies to stock options.

> **Delta** is the movement of the option value relative to the stock value. A high delta means the option price moves almost the same dollar value as the stock price. Of interest is that the percentage of movement will be higher for the option price because the option price is a lower number than the price of the stock.[14]
>
> A similar money movement on the stock price and option price is a different percentage amount for each.

Assume you are short term trader and only interested in **owning** only options and not the underlying stock. Such a trader might buy a "deep in the money" call option (a strike price considerably below the current stock price) with a high delta **when they think the stock will increase over time**:

> 1) A short-term trader would choose the lowest strike price **call option** possible. Such an option becomes of value when the

---
[14] Note: that the delta of an option can vary over the life of the option.

strike price plus premium is reached in the underlying stock price, which should be close to the current stock price.
2) Short term traders use the concept of delta to measure how the option price will move with the stock price. Basically, if the option's delta value is high, for example a delta of 1, then a $1 change in the stock price will result in a $1 change in the option price. This means that the percentage of the option price increase will be larger than the percentage of stock price increase. As an example, if the stock price moves from $100 to $101 for a 1% increase, an option priced at $9 will increase to $10 making a little over a 10% increase. One short term approach is for a short-term investor to buy the highest delta, this means the option percentage increase will be higher than stock price percentage.
3) Short term traders might buy at 52-week low point for the price of the underlying stock, at the stock price's support point or when the fear/greed in the market is low but there is reason to believe the stock price will increase during the duration of option.
4) They might select a long-time frame option.
5) They might sell/close an option at the stock price's support level.
6) They would likely sell/close the option before expiry. The option is worthless at expiry.

Tool Tip

Delta calculators:

https://www.ivolatility.com/calc/

http://www.option-price.com/index.php

Short Term Options Strategy 2

A short-term investor who is **not interested in a stock** might do a call option credit spread, when they expect the **stock price to decrease**.

1) Assume that the stock was at high point (near its price resistance level) and is moving down.
2) The investor might **sell a call option** at the 1st higher strike price above resistance (above current price).
3) The investor might **buy a call option** at the 2nd higher strike price above current price.
4) Profit is on the profit/premium/fee between the sell and buy prices
5) Risk is if the stock goes above the 1st strike price then the investor needs to exercise a purchased call option at the 2nd strike price. If the stock price goes up above the 1st strike price then loss is the difference between two strike prices minus profit.
6) If stock starts to go up to resistance line then the investor would close both options.

Short Term Options Strategy 3

A short-term investor who is **not interested in owning a stock** might buy a call credit spread when the **stock price is expected to decrease.**

1) The investor might **buy a call option** with a strike price i.e. $105, above the current price (i.e. $100)
2) The investor would **sell a naked call option** below the current price i.e. $95
3) If the stock price ends at a price (P) below or equal to $95, neither option will be exercised and the total profit will be the $5 per share from the initial options trade.
4) If the stock price is at a price (P) above or equal to $105, both options will be exercised and the total profit per is equal to the sum of $5 from the original options trading, a loss of (P - $95) from the sold option, and a gain of (P - $105) from the bought option. Total profits will be ($5 - (P - $95) + (P - $105)) = -$5 per share (i.e. a loss of $5 per share). The loss is due to speculation that the price would go down but it actually did not.

Options Analysis and Strategy

There are many metrics to use to understand options such as delta, gamma, vega, and theta for your analysis.

I tend to use a simple table as follows to understand an option:

Stock	Next quarterly return date	Number of options contracts to sell/buy	How many shares do I currently have (for selling cover call options)	Expiry date of the option contract

Current stock price	Stock resistance price	Strike price	Profit (premium less transaction fees)	Implied volatility (% change that stock price must increase to reach strike price)

Figure 16: Options Analysis

Your analysis should show that:

- There is acceptable distance between the strike price and the current price.
- That the quarterly return and dividend dates won't effect the stock's price.

- You have enough shares to do a covered call.
- You consider the resistance price. Perhaps choosing a strike price above the resistance price. The resistance price is the upper price that the stock tends historically not to raise above.[15]
- The implied volatility is at an acceptable level given the strike price and our inclination to sell the underlying stock or not.

Note: Quarterly return releases could significantly effect a stock price so consider not doing an option duration that includes a quarterly return date.

As we see in the following figure, Option 1 and 2 could be used during opposite times of the market cycle when its at a high point and a low point.

Stock price expected to **decrease or be stable and you own the stock**	Stock price expected to **decrease and you want to buy the**	Stock price expected to **increase.**

---

[15] Most stock trading sites will provide calculated resistance levels. Otherwise you can look at a chart of historical values to gain a sense of the upper most price the stock has obtain over the last several months.

but want to sell it.	stock.	
sell covered calls	sell covered puts	buy stock

Figure 17: Options Strategy Summary

> **Takeaway**
>
> I strongly recommend that you practice doing options using pretend accounts i.e. not actual trading using real money. Practice to understand your selling of option strategy, when/why you would close an option call/put and how the stock or ETF that you would do options with flows and reacts to market events. Trading the options and when its best to close the option or let it be called. How options fit with what you are doing with your stocks.
>
> You might want to start with a low volatility stock or ETF. ETFs tend to have less volatility than stocks.
>
> Understand and develop your strategy before acting.

> **Takeaway**
>
> Its worth repeating:

Consider a covered call option when you **own** a stock and are ready to sell it.

In other words, its part of your sell strategy.

Consider a covered put option when you **want to own** a stock. In other words, its part of your **buy strategy**.

Never do naked options or the short-term options trading strategies mentioned in this chapter. Just be aware that short-term traders have many ways they can use options and you can benefit from their approach.

Summary

- Covered calls and covered puts can be used to decrease the cost of buying a stock. The income earned from selling the option thus lowers the amount paid for the stock and thus protects some downside protection by lowering the cost of the purchase.
- Selling covered calls and covered puts have some risk associated with them.
- A covered put can be sold when you want to own a stock and suspect it will go down in price during the duration of the option.
- A covered call can be used when you own the stock and are comfortable with selling

some of the stock linked to a covered call option.
- Consider a covered call option when you want to sell some stock.
- A cover call option could be used as your part of your sell strategy. Once you have decided to sell a stock then use the cover call approach to earn some more income before the stock is sold.
- It's worth understanding how short-term investors use options but their strategy isn't aligned with our long-term approach. However, it does suit our long-term strategy to repeatedly sell them covered options.
- Don't do naked call or put options.
- Don't be greedy choosing strike prices.
- Practice doing options using pretend money to understand how they work and what your strategy will be.
- Don't rush it, take your time and be sure what and why you are selling an option.

"The major fortunes in America have been made in land." John D. Rockefeller

Chapter 12 Real Estate

Real estate is an interesting alternative investment to stocks. In this chapter we discuss buying property and renting it to others. There appears to be a trend to renting rather than buying a house for many people. As the possibility of house ownership for people falls then the renting becomes a growing industry.

There are many forms of developed real estate that can be rented such as office buildings, apartments, and single-family houses. In addition, undeveloped land can be used to earn income perhaps until the land is at an optimal value for development. For example, putting a mini golf course on the land or a tree farm or a bee colony or renting it to local food growers.

Leaving the land undeveloped and renting it could be seasonal or have inconsistent usage but doesn't have the complexity or maintenance issues of a house. Office buildings and apartments, even small apartments, have a level of complexity beyond a beginner stage. For the purpose of this book we will focus on single family houses. Bigger opportunities such as apartments have similar basic concepts and additional ones around overall building maintenance, for example, elevators. Multiplex houses have a potential bigger ROI due to multiple income streams within one building.

There are two basic ideas of return on investment from real estate investing:

1) Not everyone can afford the down payment and has the financial structure for obtaining a loan/mortgage for real estate. The real estate investor is providing that financial starting point. Over time, starting from the initial down payment, the remaining cost of the real estate (including buildings) is paid for by tenants/renters. This should mean a multifold profit over time with little risk.
2) A rental property brings in rental income which is a revenue stream for the investor.

Each region is different in its population composition and different legal jurisdictions have different legal and tax implications for rental property. We definitely want to research local market conditions, and, legal and tax implications. For example, some regions have rental rate increase restraints.

Tenant Profile

The tenant target market for a single-family home are apartment renters that would like to live in a house. In general, applicants looking to rent a house aren't those in the market to buy a house but tend to be renters who might consider either an apartment or single-family house. In general, many such individuals would prefer a house given that its cost is comparable to an apartment.

Recommendation 8

Look for a smaller house, perhaps a 2 story 3-bedroom townhouse, that will have a comparable rent cost to an apartment.

With a larger house, the potential house appreciation might be higher but the tenant population could be different. If one is able afford to rent a bigger house, they might also consider buying their own smaller house. The focus is on apartment renters as applicable individuals looking for a house. So, the rental cost needs to be similar to an apartment rental cost but with the added features of a house.

It's a Business…

Owning a rental property is similar to managing a business and needs to be managed using proper documentation, record keeping and attention to details that need to be done. Part of this process can be done by a professional property manager. A property manager should have a reliable process for finding and validating tenants, monitoring house use and dealing with issues. While its tempting to save the money and do property management yourself, at least initially consider the expertise that a property management brings including avoidance of costly mistakes that a lack of knowledge can entail.

In many tax jurisdictions, revenues and expenses are applied to personal income tax and the selling of the house is subject to capital gains tax. Expenses include mortgage interest, property management, lawyer, welcome gifts to tenants, and repairs. Keep receipts of all these expense items and claim them against your rental income.

But Treat Tenants Well

Generally, it costs money to have tenants leave and obtain a new tenant so its worth doing the right thing to keep tenants happy[16]. As well, keep in mind the impact you are having on other people, always treat people (tenants) well. In apartments, tenants have to follow processes, rules and bureaucracy that doesn't care much about them so a combative attitude can develop.

An attraction of being in your rental property is that you care about the tenants as individual people.

When a tenant leaves consider collecting a testimonial from them about the care provided to them to put on your description of the house.

---

[16] In jurisdictions that have rent control, the tenant leaving is a time to adjust the rent to the prevailing rate.

New House and Upgrades

I suggest you buy a new house. Old houses are buying someone else's problems and could need renovations. Unless you understand renovations, they add uncertainty to the expenses and time to do which could take away from having the house rented. It's possible to do the renovations yourself but there is uncertainty around the extent of renovations needed and home inspections might not reveal all the renovation issues.

Upgrades should be on reducing future maintenance costs such as hardwood/laminate floors instead of carpets.

Another factor to consider for upgrades is what makes the house more attractive to renters. Are there options that will make the space more inviting, friendly and home like for tenants, such as storage space, appliances (air conditioning), and neutral colors? Ensure that the kitchen, bathrooms, and bedrooms are attractive.

Buy/Sell

Generally, we can hold property indefinitely and even pass it along to family or other people. However, we can deploy the cycle concept described earlier in this book to set some considerations as to when to buy or sell. Understanding the local rental and economic conditions helps to establish an understanding of the market for rental properties. For example, some regions focus on intensification plans for housing that might create an opening as more apartments could mean more individuals looking for the opportunity for a house.

Buy when the market is weak i.e. interest rates might be high or the economy might be down. In such an economic situation, new housing development might be down and people can't afford to purchase a house.

Sell when the market is strong i.e. interest rates might be low and everyone is looking to buy. Low interest rates tend to mean a movement from apartments to self owned properties.

Return on Investment from Real Estate

Return on Investment comes from the appreciation value of the house and the payment of the mortgage accomplished through the rental income. The gain on your original down payment and the selling price are capital gains.

Once the mortgage is eliminated then the rental income is added to Return on Investment. Figuring out Return on Investment is complex due to the number of variables involved but generally in a relatively normal real estate market, a conservative estimate is 5-10% a year including taxes. This return can vary given many factors including location and local economic conditions.

However, consider a historical comparison to the S&P 500 index. Taking into account, dividends, rental income, etc., we see that between 1975 and 2014, the index averaged 10% per year while real estate average 11.5% a year. The small difference might not be much for a particular year, but as we have seen in an earlier chapter, the compounded difference over time is significant.

Approximate Ratios

In my experience, I have found the following approximate expense related ratios:

> Property manager – 1 month's rent for finding tenant and then 7-8% per year for managing.
>
> Maintenance reserve – 3-5% per year.
>
> Property tax – 1% per year.
>
> Tenant property insurance - .4% per year.
>
> Mortgage payments – depends on several factors.

An acceptable rental cost can be researched by looking at local rental rates for similar rental houses and apartments. My experience has been that the rent cost per month would be approximately 1/2% of the house purchase cost. Obviously in your region the rates could be different.

Property Maintenance Policy

When to do maintenance? As discussed earlier, caring for the well being of the tenants is a primary goal. The urgency and impact of the maintenance repair is what should be considered when considering the amount of time to fix it.

Emergencies (water leaks, fires, electrical panel issues) should be addressed immediately. If issue impedes on the usability of the property (like a refrigerator that isn't cooling, or broken door lock) than it should be addressed as soon as possible.

It should also be addressed as soon as possible if the issue could cause damage to another area in the property (like peeling/cracking caulking around a bathtub or caulking around the windows or eavestroughs leaking).

Cosmetic issues like cracks in the drywall or paint flaking on baseboards or a floor plank that is slightly lifting, can be addressed at your discretion.

Cycles in Real Estate

Most real estate developers plan their development projects years in advance and thus might be misaligned with the current state of the economy. In other words, they might bring a new development into the market when the economy is down, although they might try to delay a project if possible. Consider looking to buy during periods in the economy when a recession has hit or people are worried about their jobs and less likely to buy a house.

Consider approaching a developer towards the end of the calendar year or real estate project when they are looking to sell their remaining inventory. They might not lower the price but you might be able to obtain free upgrades.

When interest rates or housing prices move to a low or high point that might spark a move to buy or sell. That might mean its worthwhile to buy after the initial flood of buying. When interest rates go down there will tend to be a flood of pent up buying demand so consider moving to buy or sell before or after that pent-up demand is released.

Recommendation 9

For new real estate projects, developers tend to need to have sold 25% of the development sold before financing agencies are willing to lend them money. Thus, developers might have special offers available if you are able to buy early and wait awhile before development is completed. If necessary, a real estate mortgage agent who is linked into new development information sources to be on the watch for such opportunities.

Your Team

Your support team should consider of:

- A mortgage broker or provider
- Real estate lawyer
- House renovator
- Property manager
- Real estate agent or broker

Start by asking around your friends and family to get a referred individual on the above list. Once you find one of the individuals mentioned above and you trust them, likely they can recommend the other team members. For example, a property manager is likely to have a preferred renovator for their clients. Thus, when working with that renovator that works with your property manager, you are part of a larger group of clients associated with the property manager and therefore, the renovator doesn't want complaints to get to the property manager.

Summary

- Real estate investing is a relatively risk free investment where you can use your financial capability to place the initial funding requirement and then over time a renter effectively buys the property for you.
- Your first priority is figuring out how to create a positive environment for the renter. Treat people well and they will take care of your place.
- A rental property needs to ensure that the management/business aspects of it are done well.
- Consider buying and selling dependent on the cycles in the market.
- Establish who will be your renters and then create the environment that works for that type of renter. For example, a family has different needs then a single individual.
- Don't buy an older home unless you know renovation processes and costs.
- Look for the opportunity to design (i.e. a new home) so that maintenance cost is minimized.
- Build a trust team of advisors.
- Buy and sell when its opportune given the state of the economy and a real estate developers life cycle for a new development.

"I skate to where the puck is going to be, not where it has been." Wayne Gretzky

Chapter 13 Start-up Companies

Investing in start-up companies is an interesting way to get in early on the potential of a theme and a particular company. Not all companies are listed on the public stock exchange, some are privately owned by pension funds, angel investors, venture capitalists, asset management companies, etc. This type of funding and ownership is called private equity. Angel investors (also called dragons) are individuals with sufficient wealth to be able to invest funds in a start-up and potentially lose money if the start-up doesn't succeed.

Startup companies can be riskier than a company listed on the public stock exchange. Companies listed on the public stock exchanges have to fulfill regulatory requirements on reporting while there is less requirements for start-ups.

Over the last decade or so, the number of companies listed on the public stock exchange has dropped approximately in half while private equity capital going into start-ups has increased. There is significant focus on start-up companies and the opportunities they represent.

Investing in a start-up is a good way to capture the significant portion of return on investment. When a company is listed on the public exchange there are still potentially profits to be made but in some cases most of the gain occurs when the company is in its pre public stock exchange listing stage.

Investing in a start-up is somewhat different than the public stock market companies, for example as mentioned earlier, legislative protection around communication and reporting differ. Indeed, much of the rigorous regulatory oversight for private market companies is weaker or not present for start-ups particularly around reporting and standards for accounting. As such, due diligence is different and perhaps more important as you need to really feel confident in the management team and the opportunity.

Finding a Start-up Company

Most regions have angel investor associations, perhaps start-up incubators/accelerations and other start-up support associations. This is a good place to start to find start-up opportunities. Attending local start-up events is a good way to begin connecting with start-up opportunities and knowing who the people are in the industry that have a trust reputation.

I don't use online sites that have lists of start-ups looking for funding, its too easy for scams to surface on those sites. In addition, it's not a positive indication that the start-up team can't find funding unless they list on such a site rather than within their local network. Similarly, start-ups that send unsolicited offers to people outside their normal network or region are suspect.

Takeaway

Note that many start-ups aren't worth investing in. You will see many weak (not worth investing in) opportunities and few viable ones. In fact, be ready to say no to opportunities many more times then you will say yes.

Don't invest in any opportunities that are discussing alternative share arrangements such as initial coin offerings and other forms of trading your money for a dubious connection to the start-up.

Its either shares for the investment money or debt that is convertible to shares upon a predetermined event occurring such as the company being bought out by another company.

Investing

Typically, start-up companies have several rounds of investment. As start-up companies can have several rounds of investment consider having money available to participate in future rounds.

Start with the minimum investment amount, don't invest beyond that amount no matter how exciting the opportunity seems.

The principle of diversifying that we saw with public companies applies even more so to start-ups. Its better to have a smaller position in different start-ups which are in diverse industries than investing all your money in one start-up. A concentrated portfolio of significant investments can seem attractive given their profit benefit but start-ups inherently have higher risks and thus significant investments in an individual start-up is not advisable.

Never buy into the hype that a particular start-up will be the next (and only) super star, there are many, many start-up opportunities. As society and the economy change there will be many new opportunities and types of opportunities in the future.

If the investment is in the form of debt convertible to equity, the potential market for the start-up should be large and have established companies that might be interested in buying the start-up.

The start-up should have enough financing and a validation approach of all the assumptions inherent in its business plan.

First Steps:

Begin with an investable theme and then pick the company that can best realize that theme. Always ensure your start-up investment is aligned with one or more of your themes.

Then gain access to the management team and meet with them.

As discussed below, if for some reason the CEO/President and executives are not available for you to meet then don't invest.

A key indicator is your assessment of the management team. The founding and executive team should be experienced in start-ups and the market/industry space that the product/service is in. The team should always be willing to talk to you about everything they are doing. This is an advantage of investing with a start-up as opposed to investing in a public stock market company, complete access to the management team and insider information.

Factors to Evaluate the Start-up Company

Start-ups are complex entities with many assumptions around financing, the management team's capability, competitor reactions, customer, market share, etc. Basically, every assumption made by the founders is a risk that might not turn out well.

Transparency – There should be nothing between you and everything about the company. You should be able to meet with the company executives and have a truthful and open conversation about themselves and their company. If information is withheld or appears to be untrue or exaggerated or has a blockage such as distance or a 3rd party spokespeople that doesn't allow for that conversation, then don't invest. There might be some information which in the order of privacy can't be shared, for example, issues around personal privacy.

Moat – There should be barriers to entry that the start-up can create, such as economies of scale, brands, network effect and intellectual property such as patents. Patents typically involve solving complex problems. Consider not investing if competitors can readily copy the company's offering and customers see no value in brand loyalty. This typically excludes tangible products which can be low cost produced. An example of this might be ride sharing companies where the switching costs of both customers and drivers is low.

Customers - The company should be able to readily connect with customers who have a problem and willing to spend on the solution. For business customers, that usually means saving money or increasing revenue. For individual consumers, that might mean aligning with their personal goals or focus in life or perhaps solving an issue in their life so the individual can then get on to focusing on their personal goals.

Consider not investing if the team relies too much on vague assumptions about connecting with customers such as assuming social media is all that's necessary. In addition, product/service offerings to individual consumers that depend on consumers arbitrarily choosing one particular solution are problematic and rely on luck.

Team – The management team should be experienced in all aspects of the company.

Don't invest if the team has ever done anything unethical.

Check the management team's capability carefully. You want a team that is well connected such they can readily establish the required partners and first customers that the company needs.

In addition, check out who are the other investors. They should be significant individuals who can support the start-up with finding customers, partners and companies interested in buying the start-up. Determine if the other investors and those on the board of advisors are smart, accomplished individuals with experience in start-ups and who have extensive experience in the industry that the start-up is in.

If you are more capable and more connected to the start-up's industry and that industry's key players, then be cautious.

Is the team adaptable? If some event occurs that isn't positive for them can they change direction, solve the situation and continue to their goal? You want a capable team who can respond to set backs and pivot direction when something isn't working.

Financial – The company should have access to the range of financing that they might need over the life cycle of the company.

Consider not investing if financing and profitability is viewed as being of minor importance.

Understanding - If you don't understand their business model, technology, customer, product, etc. *then consider not investing.*

Testing the Business - The premise of a start up is based on a whole set of assumptions. The management team should be testing each assumption by gathering real data from real customers. For example, what will customers pay for the product, how often will they use it, how can we describe the typical customer? Management should have a plan that tests each assumption and adapts the company accordingly until they have proven that the business is viable.

Assumptions are typically future oriented and are estimates, while facts are typically past oriented and validated by external reliable sources. Each non-fact established assertion in the start-up plan is an assumption that needs to be tested.

Typically, we can segment this testing into three broad segments.

> First, is the product/service viable i.e. can it be built according to requirements which include cost and quality?

> Second, are the competition and customer assumptions, such as the price, profits, promotional, market estimates valid?

> Third, are the assumptions around scalability and growth doable?

Each of the testing segments need to be proven i.e. accomplished before financing is agreed to for the next segment.

> *Management should have a: test, gather metrics, adapt and repeat cycle mentality.*

The team should be focused on data gathering and analysis of each planned interaction with customers, partners, competitors, investors, etc.

Exit Strategy – Prior to investing you need to know how you might get your money out of the start-up. Typically, start-ups are sold to other companies or perhaps listed on a public stock exchange. In either situation the objective is to obtain shares of a publicly listed company. In the second situation, your shares of the start-up are transferred for shares of the other, publicly listed, company.

In rare cases, a company might have significant cash flow to buy the shares back from investors but this usually not feasible.

Any other approach that might see shares swapped from something else that then needs to be traded from money is suspect. For example, if the company produces wine and you will be given bottles of wine which can then be sold, or it produces bitcoins and you will be paid in bitcoins.

Summary

- **Start-ups can be an opportunity to participate in high returns, however, they have higher risks around a multitude of factors such as their inability to obtain sufficient funding, an inexperienced management team or investors, fraudulent activities, or reactions by entrenched competitors.**
- **Expect to say no to many more opportunities than yes.**
- **The founding/executive, investor and advisory team needs to be extremely capable.**
- **The start-up team should be transparent, ethical and address all your questions.**
- **Look for start-ups in your region. It's an issue interacting with start-ups that are far away.**
- **The start up needs to be evolving with specific data gathered as they test each of their business plan/model assumptions**
- **You need to know there is an exit path for you to obtain your investment and profit.**

"Know what you own, and know why you own it." Peter Lynch

Chapter 14 Gold and Silver

Gold and silver have a place in a long-time horizon portfolio.

Gold

Gold's primary two uses are as a hedge against economic/political situations and in jewelry, industrial uses for gold are not as significant.

Historically, gold was a safe haven asset during times of economic crisis or uncertainty and thus provided an inverse asset to stocks. It doesn't appear that this safe haven role is as prominent a role as it used to be. In other words, we can't reliably anticipate that the price of gold will move inversely to the stock market's stock prices in times of uncertainty. However, gold can serve as a risk reduction approach to public stock exchange stocks. While gold might not be a perfect negative to stocks it tends to not move in the same direction of the stock market or in the same percentage change. Gold can be used to reduce risk in the portfolio and as a long-term investment.

In the two figures given below, we see the historical price of gold both adjusted and unadjusted for inflation. If we consider the price of gold in 1915 as $500 U.S., in today's dollars, then gold has appreciated to about $1500 over 100 years or about $10 a year or about 2% a year on the original $500.

It wasn't until the mid 1970s that it was legal for the individual to own gold in the US so that could have had an impact on the price of gold for decades prior to the 1970s.

According my analysis of the price of gold over the last 20 years, gold has appreciated, on average, about 7-9% per year. As we see in the figures below there is volatility in the price with sometimes significant gains and drops in value but those changes tend to be of a short duration.

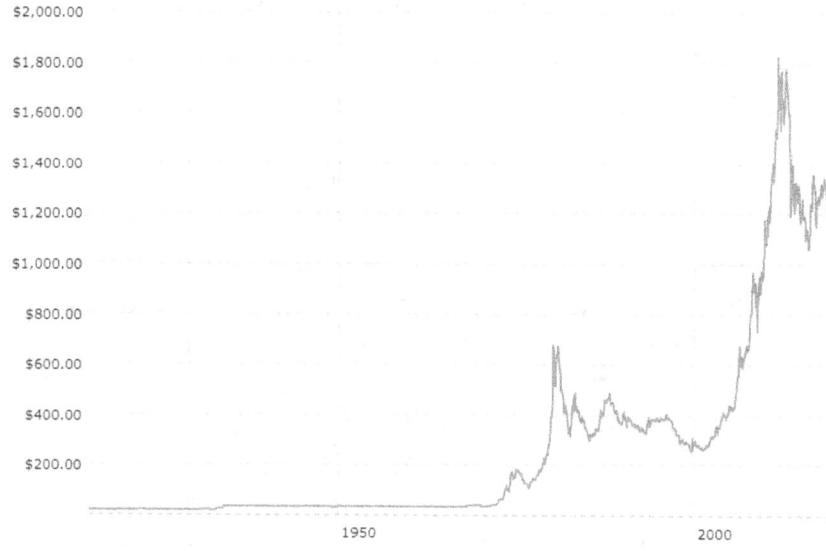

Figure 18: Historical Price of Gold

Figure 19: Inflation Adjusted Historical Price of Gold

In the following figure, we see how gold has increased on a compounded and simple average basis between 1975 and 2017 vs a house. In 1975 the average price of a house in the US was approximately $42,000 vs $160 per Troy once of gold. As we can see gold has increased over time at a rate a little higher than house prices.

	1975	2017	Compounded annual growth rate	Annual percent (straight line) growth rate
House	$42000	$287,633	4.69%	13.9248%
Gasoline	$.59	$2.41	3.41%	11.3801%
Gold	$160.88	$1,257.15	5.02%	16.2243%

Figure 20: Gold vs Houses Returns in U.S. Dollars

Gold has increased in value with the pace of houses, although its not a perfect comparison, as a house can serve as a rental property thus earning income or as a place of residence thus eliminating rent costs for accommodation. As well, houses today are different than houses of previous eras.

However, if we consider gasoline, which is relatively the same product in 1975 and 2017, we still see gold increasing faster.

In the following figure we can gain a different perspective by considering how many ounces of gold it took to buy a house in 1975 vs in 2017. As we can see, we can buy more house per ounce of gold in 2017 then 1975.

	1975	2017	Compounded annual growth rate	Annual percent (straight line) growth rate
house	262	228	-0.33	-0.3090

Figure 21: Ounces of Gold per House

Silver

Silver has a wide variety of industrial uses such as LED chips, medicine, electronics, photovoltaic (solar) energy, keyboards, televisions, batteries, cell phones, calculators, cameras, watches, clocks, and microwave ovens, RFID chips (for tracking parcels or shipments worldwide), semiconductors, touch screens, and water purification,

Silver is aligned with economic growth and the increasing computerization of the world. Only 10-15% of annual gold demand worldwide comes from industrial use while approximately 60% of silver demand comes from industrial uses.

Silver hasn't appreciated as much in value over the years as gold. A quick analysis shows silver appreciating on average over time of approximately 5% a year.

> Silver can be more volatile than gold. So anticipate that it could significantly change in value over time periods.

Gold and Silver

Gold and silver are worth considering as assets in your portfolio in small quantities. Investments in gold and silver can achieve different purposes. Together they:

- have a decent rate of return.
- provide a hedge or countermovement to public market stocks.
- are linked with economic growth in the increasing computerization of the world.
- are liquid (quick and easy to convert to cash).

We can use the concept of cycles, discussed in an earlier chapter, to purchase gold and silver when it's opportunistic.

Bullion

One way that I have seen to buy gold or silver is as bullion coins, wafers or bars, not as a collectible coin[17][18]. As a collectible coin, part of the value of the coin is intrinsic and thus, we are paying for that

---

[17] Some jurisdictions don't have a sales tax on the purchase of investment level silver or gold but do have a capital gains tax on your sale of the metals.

[18] Two ways to buy could be Canadian Maple Leaf or American Eagle coins. Look for the percentage of gold or silver in the coins, some have 99.99% purity.

intrinsic value which has an unreliable price determinant as we will see in the chapter on collectibles.

If we buy gold or silver from a retailer (gold/silver dealer), they will sell gold or silver at 2-5% above the current (spot) price of gold or silver and buy it from individuals at 2-5% below the spot price of gold or silver. Which means that if your option to selling gold or silver is to a gold or silver dealer than you always need to calculate its value as a few percentage points below the spot price of gold or silver. If you buy and sell to a gold or silver dealer then its likely costing around 5-6% to acquire it and thus it might take a few years before you are breaking even on the deal. Which suggests only considering that option if the gold or silver are near a low point.

> However, keep in mind that when buying any asset, it doesn't always immediately go up in value. A stock might also take awhile to increase in value and there is usually a buying and selling transaction fee.

Perhaps you know a relative looking to sell their gold/silver or you travel to countries where gold or silver is sold without the extensive markups by the gold/silver dealer. While the previous two options might be viable, we need to be concerned about the authenticity of the gold or silver that we buy. Without the proper test equipment its difficult to know whether you are buying real gold or silver at the quality that it is priced at.

> **R**ecommendation 10
>
> Always ensure that the gold and silver you buy is authenticated, as its too easy to fake gold/silver. Check online sites for simple (do your self) and complex (with an expert and specialized equipment) ways to check the gold/silver. For example, gold doesn't rust or float.
>
> As well, buy from a reputable dealer who, if possible, issues recognised authentication receipts.

Certificates and Streaming Companies

There are other approaches to have gold or silver as part of your portfolio.

Some investment sites also provide the opportunity to buy a certificate stating ownership of a quantity of gold or silver thus saving on the storage, securing and transporting of it. However, for the average person we are unlikely to amass large quantities where the physical possession of gold or silver will be a significant storage or transporting issue. There are two issues with such sites:

- In some cases, the gold or silver is not specifically allocated by a stamped unique serial number to named individuals. So, your gold is somewhat akin to being in a pile, in which case the certificate company could

oversell the gold or silver they have under the assumption everyone won't want their gold at the same time. Thus, you might not have a clear title to a specific set of gold or silver.
- Look to determine the liquidity of the certificates i.e. trading volume. Are the certificates/units traded in such volumes and frequency that selling your gold or silver certificate won't be an issue?

Another option is to buy shares of a gold or silver streaming company. Such companies provide required financing to a gold or silver mining company in exchange for a share of the gold or silver discovered. At some mining sites there can be a mix of metals in the ground, for example, the mining company might be interested in copper and not interested in other metals found. A streaming company provides the financing, takes a share of the metals of interest, stores the metals until market conditions are right and then sells the metals on the market. For example, a gold streaming company might take their financing repayments in gold and then sell the gold when its price is high. Gold or silver streaming companies usually pay dividends and might be priced low when the stock market is high i.e., they have a low beta[19]. It might be worth considering buying shares of a gold (or silver) streaming company

---

[19] A low beta means that stock doesn't closely move with the movements of the overall stock market. Low beta companies might still see a price decrease when the overall market declines but not as much. Thus, offering some downside protection from a recession.

when the price of gold or silver is low and the streaming company's share price is low.

Summary

- Gold, over the last few decades, has averaged a 7-9% return on investment.
- Silver has averaged around 5% return on investment over the recent decades
- Generally, it does appear worthwhile to hold a small amount in gold (or silver), as a somewhat negatively correlated asset to stocks and aligned with the economy.
- There are three viable approaches to investing in gold or silver: physically holding gold or silver; buying shares in a gold or silver streaming company; buying a gold or silver ownership certificate (although its less desirable than the other two options).
- For physically holding gold or silver it's suggested to hold it in bullion (bars, wafers, etc.) rather than a collectible coin such as commemorative coin or circulated coin.
- Always check the authentication of and liquidity of selling the gold or silver. Know how you are going to sell the gold or silver before buying it.
- Ensure that you have clear title to the gold or silver which might not be the situation when buying unallocated gold or silver for a certificate.

- If possible, look for gold or silver that is individually stamped with a serial number that its issuer will provide traceability.
- Remember the spread between what you can buy gold or silver for and what you will sell it for in a retail environment could be around a negative 5%.

"On the other hand, investing is a unique kind of casino — one where you cannot lose in the end, so long as you play only by the rules that put the odds squarely in your favour."
Benjamin Graham

Chapter 15 Coins, Stamps and other Collectibles

While investing outside the stock market helps steady the portfolio from the volatility of the stock market and provide an alternative investment possibility, collectibles are a questionable alternative investment.

Collectibles were a quite a focus for the baby boomer generation. In that era there were not many ways that one could invest. An individual's home was their primary investment. Collectibles or perhaps a cottage then became that generation's secondary investment. Possibly many of the collectibles were items people obtained in their daily activities such as silver coins, trading cards, antiques, plates, comic books and stamps. Perhaps they viewed collecting as a hobby and perhaps were personally interested in the stories associated with the collected object.

However, the world has significantly changed:

- There are many opportunities to invest that weren't possible in a previous era.
- Post offices and coin mints produced so many stamps and coins including special editions that the market was flooded with stamps and coins. For many stamp editions it's possible to have millions destroyed and still millions of that edition's stamps will remain. The oversupply of items is also found with other collectibles such as comics or plates.
- The modern generation doesn't have the space in their home for antiques, china dish sets and large stamp collections.
- The modern generation is interested in collecting experiences which typically can be represented and kept digitally.

Unless a coin or stamp, etc. is of extreme rarity, in general, they are not worth investing in. The market for collectibles, that the average person collects, is shrinking. My conversations with stamp and coin dealers suggest that rare special coins and stamps and other "investible" collectibles still have a market, but the items have to be very special and of high quality.

The issues with "investable" collectibles are:

- They are illiquid and could take time to sell, such as expensive wines or art.
- In general, they need to be cared for, perhaps insured and secured.
- Their value can be largely intrinsic, in other words, their value is how another person feels about the item. If an item is in favor with the market then its value can be high. However, consider documents written or owned by historical figures. The public's perception of that historical figure could transform almost instantly as they are re-evaluated with today's morals, as such their items can go from being sought after to the bargain bin in a day.
- There is a great deal of fraud happening in the collectibles market. Without special equipment or knowledge, it might not be possible to discern the fraud.

In general, while collectibles could be an alternative investment type, they are too problematic for the average investor.

Indeed, a rudimentary analysis showed that the prices of (not "investible") collectibles such as old silver coins and old stamps either declined in value over several decades or remain somewhat consistent in price over the decades. In other words, they didn't even keep pace with inflation.

Given the issues involved and that collectibles don't align with the long-term theme of this book, we don't include them in the portfolio.

Summary

- **The value of a collectible is largely intrinsic and thus can fluctuate it depends on finding someone willing to pay for the item.**

- **Collectibles that the average person might collect such as coins and stamps appear to be in a declining market.**

- **High quality and rare collectibles might still be of value to acquire but due to their issues it's generally not recommended acquiring.**

"Opportunities come infrequently. When it rains gold, put out the bucket, not the thimble"
Warren Buffett

Chapter 16 Bonds

Bonds as an asset class, for the purpose of this book, are debt instruments issued by the government and corporations for the organization to raise money. Bonds pay interest and might be backed by an asset or maybe just the assurance that the organization will meet its obligations as in the case of U.S. treasury bonds. They range in risk from low risk US government treasury bonds to high risk junk bonds.

Bonds have two aspects:

1) Yield - which is the interest rate of the bond.
2) Price - which is the cost to purchase the bond.

Yield and price move inversely to each other. Assume an interest rate of 10% and a price of $5 for a bond, we will label as Bond A. If other bonds of a similar nature are paying a higher interest rate, for example, 11%, then the price of Bond A will need to drop, otherwise no one would buy it. Why would one buy Bond A where its yield is lower than the yield of other similar types of bonds? So, raising interest rates usually means that the price of the bond drops.

Bonds, typically (as in the case of public debt), are not an ownership claim on an asset that generates income but a promise to repay the principle in a specific currency. That currency could decrease in value over time while typically a company's stock should increase in value over time. If we buy $100 bond for 4% interest and close the bond in 5 years the principle ($100) returned doesn't have the same purchasing value as it did 5 years earlier. Our interest returns of 4% has to take into account the depreciating cost of inflation. As described earlier the price of a bond will vary depending on the prevailing interest rates so reality isn't quite as simple as described in the example. However, bonds are an income stream attached to a promise while a stock is a potential income attached to a potentially appreciating asset.

Bond yields have an inverse relationship to the stock market, bond yields tend to increase when the stock market goes down. This is why bonds are typically considered to be a worthwhile investment. It's an inverse asset to the stock market and thus provides a downside risk safeguard for when stock market returns decline.

However, while bonds and stocks differ in terms of risks, particularly within each type of the two asset types, their return has also differed over the years.

Returns: Stocks vs Bonds

Historically, bonds as an asset class generated an annual average return of 5.8% from 1926 through 2009. Stocks, as an asset class, generated an annual average of 11.8% between 1926 and 2009.

Let's look at the return potential between bonds and stock from another time period.

> Between 1959 and 2008 stocks generated on average 9.2% per year, while, bonds averaged an annualized return of 6.5%.

> Since 1926, large company stocks have returned an average of 10% per year; long-term US government bonds have returned between 5% and 6%

As we saw previously in the book, each percentage point difference per year has a significant compound difference over time.

Let's assume that we invest $1 in 1925 in stocks and $1 in bonds. By 1995 the cumulative amount in the bond and stock asset classes is substantively different. By 1995, we have accumulated $3,425.25 in our stock asset class. However, $1 invested in long-term U.S. corporate bonds grew to $44.15 during the same period. A $1 investment in long-term U.S. Government Treasuries increased to $30.68.

Looking at the long term, a study by researcher professor Jeremy Siegel shows U.S. stock equities produced a yearly return between 1802-2002 of 6.6% while U.S. bonds produced a return of 3.6% and U.S. treasury bills of 2.7% (all numbers after inflation).

According to the study this means that the purchasing power increase of buying stocks over the centuries was $700,000 for a 1 dollar invested in 1802 while for bonds it was just under $2000.

The aforementioned are U.S. examples, however consider the global economy has grown by 3% a year over the last 100 years.

Risk: Stocks vs Bonds

If over time stocks significantly out perform bonds what is the risk factor difference? In his book Siegel wrote "…investors will see that uncertain inflation will make their portfolio allocations depend crucially on their planning horizon."

In the following figure, Siegel examines different holding periods for stocks vs bonds and he concludes the likelihood for negative returns for stocks is always lower at around the 10-year holding period. In addition, the likelihood for higher returns for stocks is always higher than bonds.

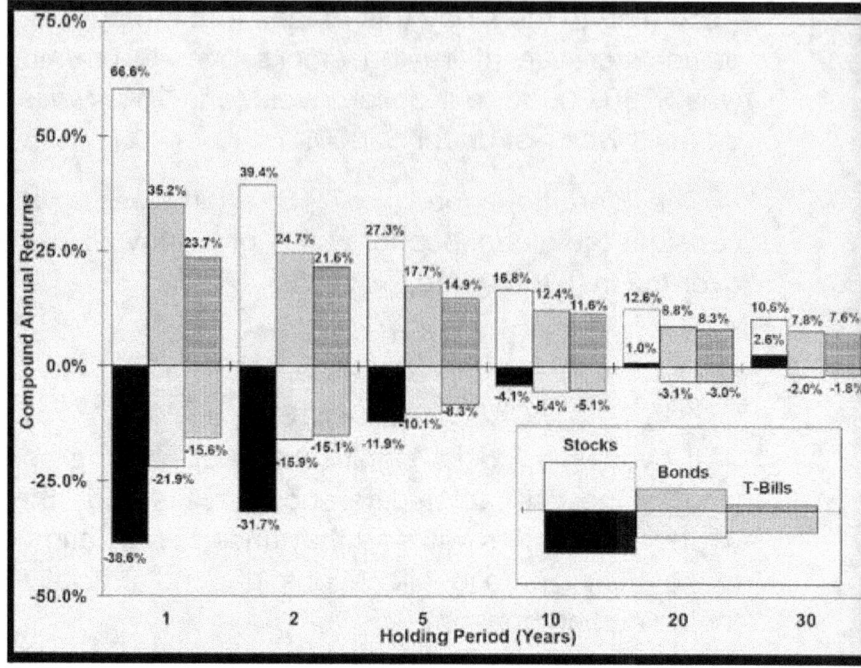

Figure 22: Stocks vs Bonds Return

(Source: Siegel, 2014)

In the following figure, Siegel demonstrates that "The standard deviation of average returns falls nearly twice as fast for stocks as for fixed-income assets as the holding period increases."

In other words, the risk of stocks decreases quicker than the risk of bonds to the point where over the 10-year holding point the risk of stocks moves lower than the risk of bonds. In his calculations he shows that that the random walk hypothesis doesn't appear to hold as results come in lower than the random walk hypothesis would predict[20].

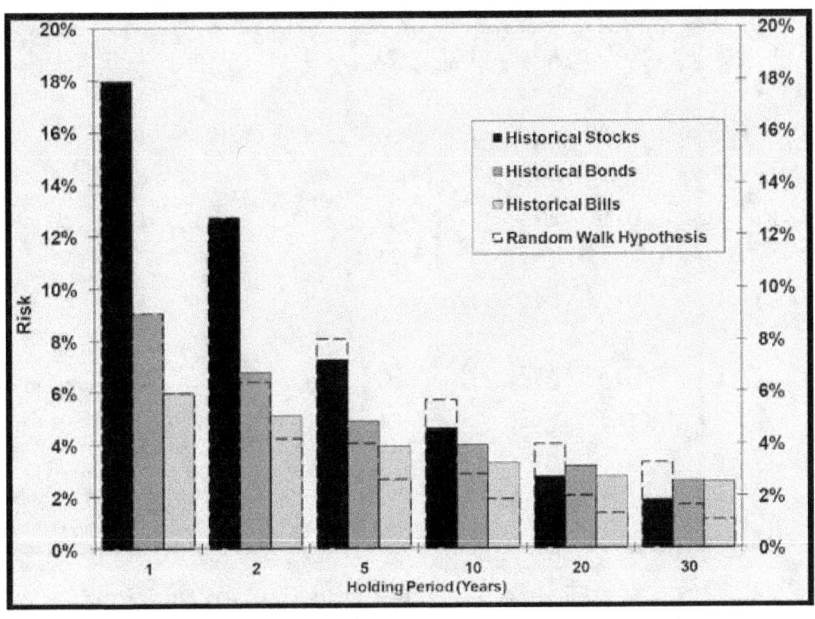

Figure 23: Stocks vs Bonds Risk

(Source: Siegel, 2014)

In the following figure, Siegel maps returns, risk and holding periods. Risk is measured as standard deviation which isn't necessarily the same as loss. His figure demonstrates that as the time horizon increases then it makes more sense to have a higher allocation in stocks. Siegel's work provides us with the insight that stocks provide a greater return than bonds over the longer time horizon and with less risk.

---

[20] The random walk hypothesis is a financial theory stating that stock market prices evolve according to a random walk and thus cannot be predicted. It is consistent with the efficient-market hypothesis.

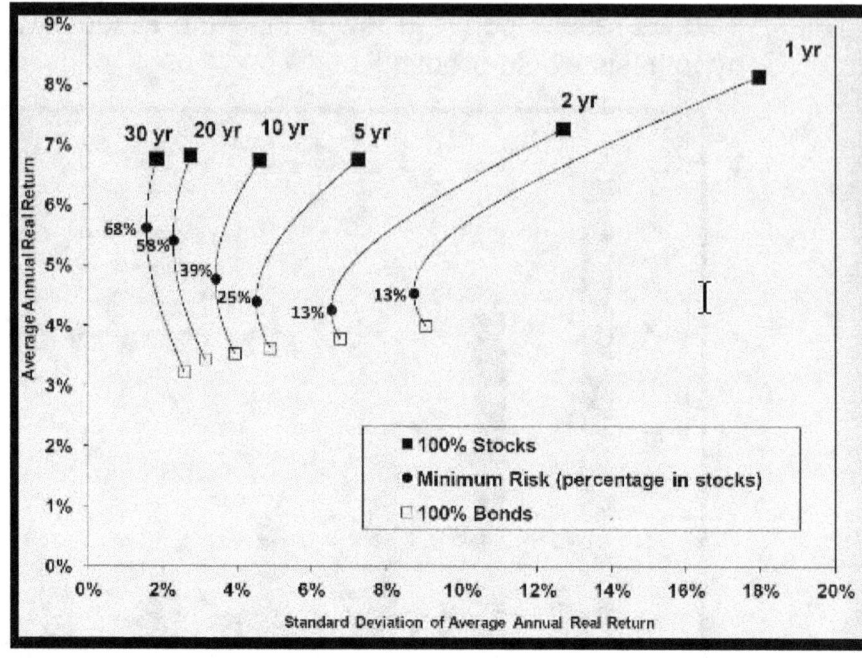

Figure 24: Risk and Return vs Time

(Source: Siegel, 2014)

Investing in bonds is recommended by many financial advisers as a way to offset the risk and volatility of stocks. However, since we are long term investors, and stocks outperform bonds in both risk and return over a long-time horizon then for the purpose of this book, we don't add bonds to our investment strategy.

Consider obtaining financial advice from a professional before making your allocation between bonds and other assets decision.

Near Substitutes for Bonds

Bonds provide an alternative income stream which is good for diversification. So consider adding *bond-like* income streams to your portfolio and/or achieve diversification in other ways as discussed in this book.

There are other ways to have an alternative investment income stream and downside risk protection arising from stocks other than using bonds.

For example:

> **Stocks** that pay a dividend rate similar to a bond, consider a stock that pays 1-3% dividend and has growth potential. A dividend paying stock is likely still correlated to the market[21] but its still an income stream if the market as a whole decline.

> **REIT** – A Real Estate Income Trust is a company that owns, and in some cases operates, income-producing real estate. They typically pay dividends and their stock will tend to act inversely to the overall stock market or at least be less correlated. Check for a REIT that has a low beta value and its in a growth phase.

> **Alternative Asset Management Companies** create a pool of different investment types such as stocks and bonds (and other interest income investments), real

---

[21] The lower a stock's beta value the less correlated it is to the marker. However, not that all stocks tend to become correlated to the market the market as a whole declines.

estate, master limited partnerships, private equity, and more. Alternative asset management companies typically have a balanced portfolio of investments, some of which are negatively correlated, in other words, their portfolio could provide an economically neutral income stream.

Indeed, some alternative asset management companies are experts on financing debt of companies, convertible securities and other interest-bearing debt. Thus, incorporating debt income streams into their approach. Asset management companies pay a dividend and some attempt to maintain a consistent return on investment comprised of capital growth and dividends.

Preferred Shares are a hybrid between bonds and common shares of a company. Preferred shares are dividend focused. Preferred shares are equity but have no voting rights. Preferred shares pay dividends. Typically, if the dividend is suspended for a while, the amount continues to accrue and needs to be repaid when dividends are re-instated. Typically, preferred shares have little volatility and tend not change much in price. Preferred shares are rated by credit agencies and typically have a lower rating than a bond since a bond is a higher obligation on the company than a preferred share.

However, a preferred share has a higher priority on the corporate assets than common shares in the event of a bankruptcy. When interest rates rise, the value of the preferred stock declines, and vice versa. There isn't the upside potential from the growth of the company that we would have with common shares. Like common shares, preferred shares are also available in ETFs.

Summary

- **Bonds have unique attributes associated with their yield and price.**
- **Bonds can act inversely to the stock market and can provide growth when the stock market declines. Historically their place in a portfolio as to serve as negative correlated asset type to stocks.**
- **Stocks tend to outperform bonds in terms of return on investment and risk as the time horizon increases.**
- **Opportunities similar to interest bearing investments can be added through dividend stocks, real estate, gold/silver, REITs, preferred shares and asset management companies. Although, such investments might not be completely buffer stock market downturns and could also suffer a turndown when stocks do as a group.**
- **Consider whether you want to add bonds as your portfolio or not. The longer your**

time horizon and more certainty around when you will need money from your portfolio then the less need for bonds.

"It is impossible to produce superior performance unless you do something different from the majority." John Templeton

Chapter 17 Currency

Currency trading is a specialized investment strategy. Typically, currency traders focus on small differences between the rates of a basket of currencies.

This is an asset class in which its difficult to be different from short term traders.

Currencies trade in comparison to each other.

A company's stock price over time would be expected to increase as the company prospers. In contrast currencies tend to fluctuate within upper and lower bands and thus years later can be within a similar price range as they were years before. While currencies should reflect the growth and potential of a country, currencies can be impacted by political events and government actions.

Therefore, currencies are not really suitable for long term investment. Most currency investors are really day traders and studies show most lose money.

A simple currency strategy might be to purchase an ETF such as FXF or similar ETFs. Typically, the ETFs are uninsured which implies an additional risk to the investor. Typically, such ETFs don't pay any type of dividend. However, by using the FXF ETF, options could be bought and options sold on it to make money.

However, for the purposes of the long-term strategy discussed in this book, we don't include currency holdings in the portfolio, that includes cryptocurrencies.

Summary

- Currencies trade in comparison to other currencies and generally over the long term, within an upper and lower band.

- Currency trading tends to be the focus of short time horizon investors and thus saturated with algorithms, thus not suitable for the average investor.

- We wouldn't include currency trading within our long-term portfolio strategy.

"In the long run, it's not just how much money you make that will determine your future prosperity. It's how much of that money you put to work by saving it and investing it."
Peter Lynch

Chapter 18 Integrated Strategy

In this chapter, we discuss the integration possibilities of investment strategies.

Investment Layers

Of the four types of investments we have discussed in the book as appropriate for a long-term investment approach i.e. stocks, options, gold, real estate and start-up companies, we need a progressive approach to investing with a starting investment type and movement to the highest level of investing type. Referring to the following figure, the starting point is stocks.

$0-$50,000

Typically, stocks are a good point to start, as available on the public stock exchange. They have some regulatory protections for the investor built into the reporting and filing requirements. While somewhat arbitrary, I see beginning with stocks until your portfolio is at least $50,000. This will give you familiarity with cycles, and analysis techniques since there are publicly available market analysts reports that you can read to compare your analysis results to.

Your goal is to practice your analysis techniques until you have confidence in picking themes and associated companies. As well, that you have controlled your emotional responses to stock market cycles and are investing in a rational thoughtful approach.

We can diversify and lower the risk of the portfolio by buying some gold/silver.

$50,000-$500,000

With a portfolio between $50,000 to $500,000, it should be diverse enough and large enough that you should have some stocks suitable for selling covered call and covered put options.

Become confident in picking option durations and strike prices such that your strategy of owning or selling the underlying stock is well practiced and done in a rational way.

In other words, don't be greedy.

$500,000-$1,000,000

If you have over $500,000 in your portfolio, then a real estate purchase will comprise 10% or so of your portfolio which is a possible starting point. Develop your real estate team consisting of a real estate lawyer, real estate agent/broker, property manager, mortgage advisor, and renovator contractor. As well, develop your processes to treat the rental property as a business particularly around taxes, documentation, maintenance, income/expenses and industry trends.

Learn to treat the tenants in a caring and empathic way that makes them happy to stay in your property.

Over $1,000,000

In many regulatory environments there is a restriction on who can invest in start-up companies. The restriction could be based on factors such as earnings or net worth. In some jurisdictions it's possible to invest as a family member or friend of the start-up's founders and thus bypass regulatory requirements.

Develop your network of founders, advisors and investors who have reputations that you can trust. Learn to identify each risk (explicitly or implicitly) in the plan and how well the management team is equipped to manage the risk.

Figure 25: Investment Layers

Each of the aforementioned strategies should be worked as a composite of investments in the following layers.

1) Real estate, and gold/silver are typically low risk and can consistently earn 5-10% per year.
2) Stocks and options can inconsistently earn between 7-15% a year
3) Start-up companies can inconsistently earn between 15+% a year.

Notes:

1. Use the following formula to figure out how the portfolio value will double over time:

    72/yearly ROI rate such as 7% = number of years to double the initial investment.
    For example, 72/10% ROI per year equals a little over 7 years to double the initial investment.

2. At least 10% of your salary/wage earnings should be put in investments each year.

Measuring Success
How do we know we are doing well?

Given we are long term investors, primarily focused on emerging themes, it can be difficult to determine if a successful strategy is happening over the short period. Indeed, its not advisable to continuously measure portfolio success over the short term. Emerging long-term themes can take longer to mature than anticipated for many reasons.

You can monitor the companies in your portfolio and their industry and gain a sense as to whether the industry is growing and the management team is taking the correct decisions.

I suggest that you listen to or read the transcriptions of the earnings report as to what management has accomplished and their future guidance. Future guidance is management's thoughts on the company's future potential. In addition, some companies prepare presentation for shareholders about their industry and strategic intentions. This gives a mechanism for determining what the management team is planning and whether they have a record of achieving their plans.

Takeaway

> If the investment (management team) is achieving their objectives and is capable to manage the changes and challenges occurring in the market/industry then that's a good indicator. This can apply to a variety of investment types.

Over time you could use the average stock market return as a benchmark. The average stock market return is 7% (not counting inflation). A crude proxy is the VFV ETF. Over time you can compare your investments with the market average.

As we discussed earlier in the book, we use the following as goals.

Global - Investment opportunities should have income from local and foreign markets. Some companies have international customers, so we can hold local companies with a foreign customer base. Its not necessary to have companies that are located in foreign countries but determine whether companies have customers located in foreign countries.

Growth Oriented – The emerging theme-based approach is growth oriented, and our factors for evaluating public market companies and private start-ups are future oriented.

Consistent – A long term buy and hold might not see consistent returns on the short term but over the long term. We would then expect to see consistent returns. Repeatedly buying and selling based on market news can result in losses. We wouldn't expect to analyze returns for any period less than one year.

Diverse – The asset classes from gold to real estate tend to be diverse and within an asset class such as companies we can look to diversify across regions, industries, customers, and business models. The correlation between the asset types varies but overall are diverse as a group/portfolio. Typically, correlation measures for stocks use price as the variable which isn't a good proxy measure as its past oriented and doesn't account for different customers types, etc.

Recession/Downside/Risk Resistant - We can address some of downside risk with selling covered options and taking of profits when appropriate. As well as having diversity within the portfolio and a long-time investing time horizon.

Using Cycles to Focus on Investment Types

Given the diversity of asset types that align with a long-time horizon emerging investment theme, we can use the natural cycles of each to decide where to invest at a particular span of time.

In general, prices of assets are driven by the economy, interest rates, psychology, political tensions, future expectations, etc.

The asset types discussed in this book have differing levels of correlation with the other asset types and the economy, interest rates, etc.

By using a variety of asset types it's possible one or more of the asset types will be at a low point in its cycle when other asset types are at a high point.

Consider the asset types of:

- Gold/silver
- Private equity start-ups
- Interest rate substitutes that pay dividends such as REITs or asset management companies, or utilities
- Growth oriented capital gains public stock market companies
- Stock options
- Real estate

Then we can move our investment focus between different asset types as optimal for a cycle. For example, in the following figure we can see that when stock prices are at peak point in their cycle, we could focus investment in gold or stocks that are bond substitutes.

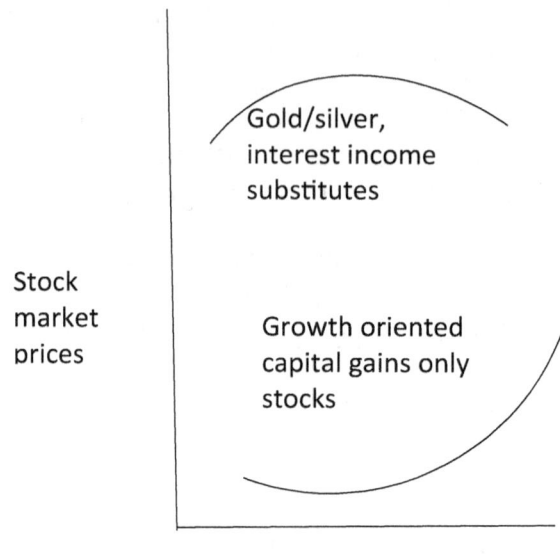

Figure 26: Deciding Investment Focus Among Asset Types

Investing as a Permanent Garden

As implied in the above figure, if we have a portfolio that is diverse its likely that some investments will be in a down position while others are up.

Think of a garden, if we want colorful flowers blooming during all available seasons, we should diversify the flower types between their different blooming seasons, sun/shade/soil conditions, etc. so that we always have some flowers in bloom. Just choosing flowers that bloom in the spring means we don't have any blooming in the autumn. Having flowers that bloom at different times of the year means some flowers are not blooming at any particular time but during the entire available season(s) we have enough blooming for a colorful garden. Our investments should be diversified such that some investments are doing well while others hibernate. We don't worry that some investments are hibernating if we are confident, they will have their turn blooming. This means that money from the blooming investments is available for harvesting when needed and money from hibernating investments will bloom when its time for the next harvest.

Takeaway

Some of your investing decisions will be wrong.

Some of your investments will lose money.

Sometimes your portfolio will be in a negative position.

Major Takeaways

Develop and maintain your watchlist of themes/trends and then assets that will implement those themes/trends. This is where most of your effort and time is spent. Do this monthly.

Constantly stress test (review) your watchlist and portfolio for its diversity and alignment with the 5 portfolio goals we saw in chapter 3. This is where the next most effort and time expenditure. Do this every 1-2 years.

Maintain 5% of your portfolio in cash and replenish when necessary.

Buy when the market is down.

Know why you will sell an asset. Sell when appropriate to your strategy not because of what the market is doing.

Buying and selling is your least most expenditure of time and effort. Indeed, it should be minimal.

Divest of your emotions.

Live frugally.

Your Portfolio's 5 Goals: Global, growth oriented, consistent, diverse, and recession/downside/risk resistant.

Keep investing.

Summary

- The asset types can form a progressive investment hierarchy that aligns with our theme based long time horizon investment strategy.
- The goals that were outlined in the beginning of the book are matched to the asset types and investment strategy.
- The diverse asset types presented in this book have a varying degree of correlation between them and other economic factors.
- We can focus on an asset type given where it is in its cycle and thus see opportunities in one asset type when none exist in another asset type.
- You need to have the financial structure to be able to move money between asset types when optimal.
- Consider whether the investment will continue is achieving its objectives and has the ability to evolve and continue to meet its objectives.
- Some of your investments will be doing well while others are in their off season or hibernating, however, overall that should balance.

"Spend each day trying to be a little wiser than you were when you woke up." Charlie Munger

In Closing

This book is meant to be both a conceptual book and to outline an approach to long term investing in several different asset types in an integrated manner focuses on emerging/growth themes. As well, the goal of the book is to be practical with ready to use ideas that you can consider for your investing strategy.

The ideas presented are for your consideration. You should also consider seeking professional advice.

Once the ideas in the book are familiar to you then the next steps are to create your emerging themes list and then watchlist of investment opportunities, for example, public stock market companies or real estate.

As well, expand your news sources so that you gain a sense of how the events of the world are connected and what trends are shaping our world.

Finally expand your network of people that can help you discover new ideas and opportunities.

Keep investing.

James Bowen

"If the job has been correctly done when ta common stock is purchased, the time to sell it is – Almost never" Philip Fisher

PART III

- Useful sites and further reading

> "It would be wonderful if we could avoid the common setbacks with timely exits." Peter Lynch

Appendix A: Sites of Interest

Understanding what the market and economy is doing. A few sites of interest are:

- RBC has macroeconomic overview summaries
    - http://funds.rbcgam.com/investment-insights/investment-outlook/index.html
    - http://media.rbcgam.com/insights/index.html
- CNN's Fear and greed indicator http://money.cnn.com/data/fear-and-greed/
- CEO's confidence in the market http://www.conference-board.org/press/pressdetail.cfm?pressid=5428 bullish or bearish
- Leading economic indicator https://www.conference-board.org/data/bcicountry.cfm?cid=1

    http://www.barchart.com/quotes/stocks/ $SMSS smart money index

- The Investor Sentiment Survey measures the

- percentage of individual investors who are bullish, bearish, and neutral on the stock market for the next six months http://www.aaii.com/sentimentsurvey?adv=yes bullish or bearish
- https://www.iif.com/publications/portfolio-flows-tracker money flows to emerging markets
- https://ca.finance.yahoo.com/advances the price advancing up or declining down
- This site gives an indication of market advisor sentiment on the stock market http://online.barrons.com/public/page/9_0210-investorsentimentreadings.html bullish or bearish
- This site gives consumer sentiment http://www.sca.isr.umich.edu/
- This site gives an indication of advisor sentiment on bonds and currency http://online.barrons.com/public/page/9_0210-boxscore.html bullish or bearish. Bonds and currency tend to operate in the opposite direction of stocks.
- US Leading[22] Economic Indicator https://www.conference-board.org/data/bcicountry.cfm?cid=1 bullish or bearish
- Europe Leading Economic Indicator
- https://www.conference-board.org/data/bcicountry.cfm?cid=10 bullish or bearish
- The bond yield curve is considered a strong

---

[22] Leading means that it's an indication of the future economic situation.

indicator of market potential[23] http://stockcharts.com/freecharts/yieldcurve.php or http://www.treasury.gov/resource-center/data-chart-center/interest-rates/Pages/TextView.aspx?data=yield a downward sloping curve is an indicator of a recession and the stock market to go down.
- The following links provide a candlestick view of stock markets, regions, and sectors which give an indication of bull and bear trends
    - http://stockcharts.com/freecharts/candleglance.html?[MARKO]
    - http://stockcharts.com/freecharts/candleglance.html?[ISHARE]
    - http://stockcharts.com/freecharts/candleglance.html?[SECT]
- This statistic shows the global Purchasing Manager Index (PMI) of the industrial sector
- http://www.statista.com/statistics/256701/global-purchasing-manager-index-pmi-of-the-industrial-sector/, if purchasing is declining it could signal that the corporate earnings will decline and thus the market.

---

[23]Yield Curve: A plot of treasury yields across the various maturities at a specific point in time. At the front (left) of the yield curve are T-Bills with maturities of 12, 26 and 52 weeks. In the middle are Treasury Notes with maturities of 2, 5 and 10 years. At the end (right) of the yield curve are Treasury Bonds with maturities of 20 and 30 years. In a normal yield curve, yields rise as the maturities increase. If the yield on shorter maturities is higher than that of longer maturities, then an inverted yield curve exists. An inverted yield curve is a sign of tight money and is bearish for stocks.

- An indicator of whether the P/E ratio is high or low can be found at:
    http://www.gurufocus.com/shiller-PE.php[24]

---

[24] There is the "Warren Buffet indicator" which he uses to determine if the stock market is too high, but I couldn't find a site that always has it updated

> *"Look at market fluctuations as your friend rather than your enemy; profit from folly rather than participate in it."* Warren Buffett

Appendix B: Sectors and Business Cycles

Sector rotation is an investment strategy that consists of moving money from one industry sector to another in an attempt to beat the market. At different stages in an economy, an investor or portfolio manager may choose to shift investment assets from one investment sector to another, based on the current business cycle (since different sectors are stronger at different points in the business cycle)[25].

A sector refers to a group of stocks representing companies in a similar line of business or industry. All of the stocks can be broken down into 12 different categories (sectors) based on their line of business or industry.

- Financials – The financial services sector is primarily banks, credit unions, insurance and mutual funds.
- Energy - The exploration, production, marketing, refining or transportation of oil and

---

[25] This appendix sourced from https://www6.royalbank.com/en/di/reference/article/stock-market-sectors-and-sector-rotation/ilsa7rci

gas products including energy related services/

- Material - Commodity type products industries such as minerals, metals, chemicals, construction materials glass, paper and forestry.
- Industrials – Aerospace, defence, construction, building, transportion such as airlines and infrastructure.
- Consumer Discretionary – Automotive, household durables, textiles, leisure. This includes services and products.
- Telecom - Internet connectivity, cable
- Information Technology – Computer hardware, software and related services
- Consumer Stables – Food, beverages, household products and personal items including retailers who supply such products.
- Utilities - Water, gas and electricity.
- Health Care - Equipment, pharmaceuticals, and related services.

Business Cycles

Early Recession – The economy begins to slow and consumer expectations are at their worst; industrial production is falling sharply, interest rates are at their highest, and the yield curve is flat or even inverted. Historically, the following sectors have profited during these times:

- Consumer staples (near the beginning)
- Health care
- Utilities (midway)

Recession – When the economy is down, industrial production is at its lowest point, people are losing jobs, interest rates begin to fall, and the yield curve is normal. Although consumer expectations are low, they are beginning to improve. The sectors that have historically performed well in this stage include:
- Consumer discretionary (near the beginning)
- Financials
- Information technology (near the end)

Early Recovery – When the economy begins to improve and consumer expectations are rising, industrial production begins to grow, interest rates have bottomed and the yield curve is either normal or has begun to steepen, the sectors to consider investing in at this stage include:
- Financials (near the beginning)
- Transportation (near the beginning)
- Industrials
- Energy (near the end)

Late/Full Recovery – At this point in the business cycle, interest rates are usually rising rapidly and the yield curve has flattened. Industrial production is slowing and consumer expectations are beginning to fall. Historically, the most profitable sectors in this stage have included:
- Energy (near the beginning)

- Materials
- Precious metals

Investor and Economic Impacts

1. Consumer Staples

Consumer non-cyclical stocks, including food and household products companies and consumer growth industries (cosmetics, tobacco, and beverages), usually receive fairly steady demand and are less sensitive to changes in the business cycle. These stocks will attract investors when the economic cycle or bull market has matured, or when the market is beginning to contract.

2. Consumer Discretionary

These stocks usually become popular when the economy is in its last stages of contraction.

3. Health Care

The health care sector is considered defensive, meaning companies in this sector are generally unaffected by economic fluctuations. The healthcare industry consists of pharmaceutical firms, biotech firms and medical equipment suppliers.

4. Financials

When interest rates are falling, stocks in housing-related industries will often do well and are popular among investors in the middle to late stages of an economic contraction. Large banks that do not depend on mortgages alone are generally helped by commercial and consumer loan growth.

5. Information Technology

Technology stocks are often cyclical. The companies depend on capital spending and business or consumer demand, which can be quite finicky. The stocks may also have long-term growth potential as new technologies are developed. Technology stocks are usually popular during early to mid stages of an economic expansion.

6. Materials

Basic industry stocks tend to receive a boost from the market late in an economic expansion. Basic materials companies are strongly affected by the global economic picture and supply/demand metrics heavily impact stock price movements.

7. Industrials

As the economy begins to improve, capital spending tends to increase as higher demand for products leads companies to expand their production capacity.

8. Transportation

Railroads, trucking companies and other surface carriers tend to react positively when the economy starts to improve. Airlines, however, are more tied to cyclical fuel costs and competitive pressures.

9. Energy

These stocks tend to be popular with investors late in the business cycle and are driven by the supply and demand picture for energy worldwide, although political events also tend to affect these industries.

10. Utilities/Telecom

Utility companies are sensitive to interest rates because of the large debt financing costs they must incur in order to build their infrastructures. These stocks tend to perform well when interest rates are declining. Telecom companies may also profit during these times.

11. Precious Metals

Precious metals (such as gold, silver, and platinum) and companies that mine and process them are largely affected by inflationary pressure and commodity price volatility. They are also affected by industrial and consumer demand. Investors often flock to this category late in the expansion cycle.

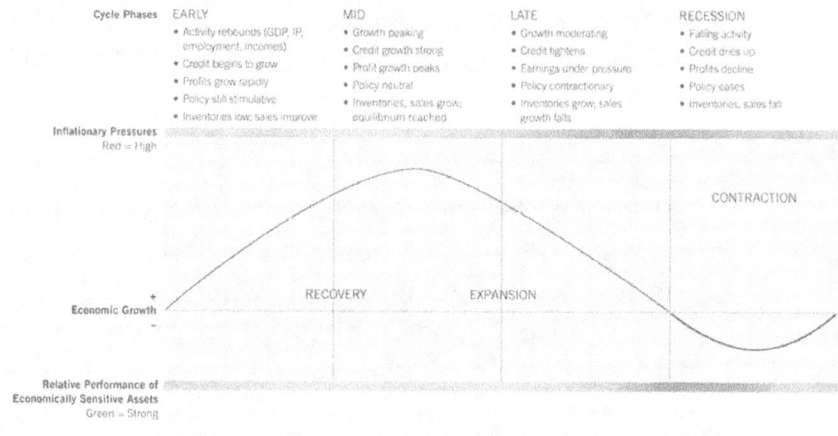

source: Fidelity Investments (AART), as of Sep. 30, 2016[26]

---

[26] https://www.fidelity.com/learning-center/trading-investing/markets-sectors/intro-sector-rotation-strats

Figure 27: Economic Sectors

"Only buy something that you'd be perfectly happy to hold if the market shut down for 10 years" Warren Buffet

Appendix C: Additional Reading

There are several legendary investors or thinks who are worth reading to learn about their investment approach, such as:

- John "Jack" Bogle
- Warren Buffet
- Benjamin Graham
- Carl Icahn
- Peter Lynch
- Howard Marks
- Charles Munger
- John Templeton
- Jeremy Siegel
- George Soros

Some books describing their investing/thinking approach include:

Benjamin Graham on Investing, Graham, Benjamin New York: McGraw-Hill, c2009., 9780071621427

Charlie Munger The Complete Investor, Griffin, Trenholme J., New York: Columbia University Press, [2015], 9780231170987 023117098X

Mastering the Market Cycle, Getting the Odds on your Side, Marks, Howard, Boston: Houghton Mifflin Harcourt, 2018., 9781328479259, 1328479250

The Bogleheads' guide to investing, Lindauer, Mel, Hoboken, New Jersey: Wiley, [2014], 9781118921289

The best investment writing selected writing from leading investors and authors. Volume 1, Petersfield, Hampshire: Harriman House, 2017, 9780857196194 0857196197

Stocks for the Long Run, Jeremy Siegel, McGraw-Hill Education, 2014, 0071800514

> *"Look at market fluctuations as your friend rather than your enemy; profit from folly rather than participate in it."*
> Warren Buffet

Glossary

B

bank	38
beta	152, 225
bonds	37, 98, 154, 218, 219, 220, 224, 225, 226, 227, 250
Bonds	36, 218, 227, 250, 251

C

cashflow	132, 152
coin	194, 208, 212, 215
collectibles	209, 214, 215, 216, 217
Collectibles	36, 214, 217
concentration	98, 108
Covered calls	179
covered put	180, 232
currency	36, 80, 229, 230, 250
Currency	36, 229, 230
cycles	24, 38, 39, 43, 80, 89, 90, 91, 109, 164, 191, 208, 232, 253

D

discounted cash flow	150

Diversification 108

E

economy ... 43, 44, 60, 61, 63, 64, 67, 68, 74, 81, 88, 90, 91, 92, 94, 96, 98, 100, 102, 105, 106, 113, 114, 126, 130, 137, 146, 150, 152, 154, 186, 249, 253, 254, 255, 256, 257

Efficient Market Hypothesis 37, 48

G

Gold 36, 106, 203, 208, 212

I

intrinsic 47, 48, 92, 146, 147, 150, 151, 209, 216

investing 7, 8, 9, 13, 24, 26, 27, 28, 29, 30, 31, 35, 36, 37, 38, 39, 40, 41, 43, 47, 49, 52, 53, 56, 62, 69, 92, 93, 94, 102, 111, 112, 116, 119, 130, 141, 145, 146, 150, 182, 191, 194, 196, 214, 215, 224, 231, 232, 244, 245, 255, 259

investor 8, 9, 36, 40, 48, 50, 52, 53, 56, 57, 58, 59, 61, 62, 69, 95, 103, 111, 137, 146, 167, 173, 174, 175, 182, 193, 201, 216, 230, 232, 253

L

legal 37, 38, 182, 204

M

Moat 134, 152, 197

O

options 36, 37, 157, 158, 159, 160, 161, 164, 165, 167, 168, 169, 170, 171, 172, 174, 175, 180, 230, 232, 235

P

Price/earnings ratio 155
Private equity 36
Private lending 36

public stock market...102, 123, 193, 196, 244
Public stock market...36

R

Real estate..36, 77, 181, 191, 235
Recession...44, 152, 255
risk......27, 29, 31, 38, 42, 44, 45, 55, 59, 62, 81, 91, 92, 94, 100, 101, 102, 103, 104, 105, 108, 109, 110, 116, 123, 136, 146, 149, 150, 151, 152, 157, 158, 167, 169, 170, 171, 179, 182, 191, 197, 218, 224, 230, 233, 235

S

Silver...36, 203, 207, 208, 212, 235, 239
stock market.....7, 37, 47, 89, 103, 104, 106, 109, 121, 146, 154, 159, 203, 214, 219, 225, 227, 232, 237, 250, 251, 252
stocks8, 37, 48, 97, 105, 123, 136, 145, 148, 150, 158, 160, 181, 203, 219, 220, 224, 225, 226, 227, 231, 232, 249, 250, 251, 253, 256, 257, 258
strategy...7, 24, 26, 31, 40, 41, 42, 45, 46, 47, 49, 50, 52, 53, 54, 57, 58, 59, 61, 62, 89, 94, 102, 111, 117, 119, 123, 130, 137, 147, 148, 149, 157, 160, 161, 167, 170, 171, 172, 174, 175, 180, 224, 229, 230, 232, 236, 244, 253
strike price159, 160, 161, 162, 164, 165, 166, 167, 168, 169, 170, 172, 174, 175

T

tax 37, 38, 169, 182, 184, 187

V

volatile...32, 104, 143, 149, 165
volatility.........49, 59, 62, 102, 103, 144, 149, 152, 166, 168, 204, 214, 224, 258

www.ingramcontent.com/pod-product-compliance
Lightning Source LLC
Chambersburg PA
CBHW070619220526
45466CB00001B/55